Nourishing Faith
Through Fiction

THE COMMUNICATION, CULTURE, AND THEOLOGY SERIES
SERIES EDITORS: PAUL SOUKUP, S.J., *and* FRANCES FORDE PLUDE

The Communication, Culture, and Theology Series publishes books that explore the theological implications of contemporary and popular culture, especially as manifest in mass or interactive media and media products. The series encourages a dialogue in which communication practices and products shed light on theology and, in turn, theological reflection deepens an understanding of communication.

Nourishing Faith
Through Fiction

Reflections of the
Apostles' Creed
in Literature and Film

John R. May

SHEED & WARD
FRANKLIN, WISCONSIN

As an apostolate of the Priests of the Sacred Heart, a Catholic religious congregation, the mission of Sheed & Ward is to publish books of contemporary impact and enduring merit in Catholic Christian thought and action. The books published, however, reflect the opinions of their authors and are not meant to represent the official position of the Priests of the Sacred Heart.

2001

Sheed & Ward
7373 South Lovers Lane Road
Franklin, Wisconsin 53132
1800-266-5564

Printed in the United States of America

Cover and interior design by Madonna Gauding
Cover Photo courtesy of Archive Photos, New York, NY
Author photo by Fred Frey

Library of Congress Cataloging-in-Publication Data

May, John R.
Nourishing faith through fiction : reflections of the Apostles' Creed in literature and film / John R. May.
      p. cm. — (Communication, culture, and theology series)
    Includes bibliographical references (p.) and index.
    ISBN 1-58051-106-6
        1. Religion and literature. 2. Motion pictures—Religious
        aspects. 3. Apostles' Creed. I.
    Title. II. Communication, culture & theology.

PN49 .M389 2001
700' .482—dc21

                         2001040089

1 2 3 4 5   04 03 02 01

For
Taylor, Jan, Julie, and John

It is above all through the Bible, the book of the Word revealed and incarnate, that God speaks, and personal contact with him is established . . . Reading it . . . becomes a personal dialogue in which the least word touches us personally.

Why does the Bible so often speak of the "living" God? Surely it is because the God it reveals to us is not the God of the philosophers, outside time and space, the origin of all things or the sublimest possible conception of the mind. He is a living person, a person whose voice breaks in upon us, who himself intervenes, who acts, who suffers, who enters into history in Jesus Christ, who enters into men by the Holy Spirit.

—Paul Tournier, *The Meaning of Persons*

Acknowledgments

Words alone would never suffice to express my indebtedness to my wife, Janet, for her enduring patience and support as she lived and worked with me through every phase of this slowly unfolding confession of our shared faith, and enjoyment of literature and film. Her beauty and devotion are "past change!"

My lifelong Jesuit friends, Walt McCauley, Tom Naughton, and Terry Todd, read all or portions of the manuscript in an earlier draft and provided invaluable encouragement and suggestions. J. J. Denniston, former Catholic campus minister at SUNY Stony Brook, now pastor of St. Patrick's Church in Huntington, New York, and faithful friend, took time off from a much-needed vacation to read with care a later draft and to offer his judicious reflections. To them all, I owe a special debt of gratitude.

I would like also to thank the students in my Catholic Doctrine course in the Religious Studies Institute of the Diocese of Baton Rouge from 1992 on, who read and commented on versions of the manuscript and eagerly shared their appreciation of my reflections on movies as well as their own fresh insights. The challenge of presenting to them an understanding of the "meaning for our daily lives" of the articles of the Apostles' Creed has been a continuing and gratifying stimulus toward revising and refining the manuscript.

On the practical side, I am especially indebted to Henry Mills, for saving the manuscript when my disk was infected with the CDEF virus; to Susan Kohler and the late Claudia Scott, for repeated technical assistance and for untold acts of secretarial kindness; and to all those in the computer services center of the College of Arts and Sciences at Louisiana State University who so graciously helped me with problems, great and small, over the past decade, and who continue to help me, especially Mark Hovey and Sachin Kamath. Even as I wonder how I ever managed to complete a manuscript without a computer, I'm humbled almost daily by the apparently basic instruction that I seem to need.

All quotations from sacred Scripture are from *The New English Bible with Apocrypha* (Oxford/Cambridge, 1970). The films recommended for viewing are available for rental at most video stores; the novels, short stories, and plays can be found in any public library.

Contents

Knowing the entire Bible by heart, and understanding it so well that you can explain every single verse, is of little use to you, unless the biblical Word penetrates your innermost being, as the rain penetrates the tiniest roots of a tree in order to rise and to fill the whole tree and to bring forth leaves and fruit.

My dear friends, how often do we fall into this very error when we read the Scriptures! We grasp what we read with our minds alone and then let it pass as hard soil lets pass a light rain. Let us employ this [time] not to explain the text, . . . but to grasp it and use it as did the woman in the parable of our Lord who took a leaven and worked it into the dough until it was completely leavened. We will ask God to work his Word into our hearts, into our lives, until they are all filled with it.

—Emil Brunner, *Sowing and Reaping*

Faith and Fiction:
An Introduction

Anyone who, like me, has lived as long before the Second Vatican Council as after, has had the experience of living in two distinctly different worlds of faith. And if one has gone from teaching religious studies in the 1960s and '70s to teaching English in the 1980s and '90s, again as I have, the sense of disparate worlds may be even greater.

The inspiration for this work is rooted in this dual experience of change. Regularly I find myself recalling two circumstances that typify my sense of shifting worlds, especially when giving talks on literature, film, and religion. The first memory is of an isolated occasion in the mid 1960s; the second situation has occurred repeatedly, or it seems as if it has, over the past two decades.

As Vatican Council II drew to a close, I was teaching theology at a small Catholic college in the South. The faculty met occasionally to discuss curricular and other matters of concern, and at that time, discussions frequently turned to the changes within the Church that were not, as some will recall, immediately accepted with open heart by everyone. The particular evening I remember vividly, we had been discussing the liturgical changes that were introduced by the council, some of which we were already implementing at the college, and our attention had focused on the reasons for the mandated changes and the implications for the future of reform. I recall that during the discussion I made what I considered at the time, and even more so now, a pertinent observation about the need for the signs and symbols of the liturgy to be self-explanatory, and I used an obvious example from the Eucharist itself. I pointed out how needlessly complicated we had made our catechesis for Communion by using flat, round wafers. Children had to be told that the host was bread because it looked like nothing they had ever associated with bread. If Jesus broke bread at table and gave it to his disciples, and this was what we were supposed to be doing in remembrance of him, I went on to say, flippantly to be sure, our communion service—of wafer placed on extended tongue— was more a memorial of Jesus' commanding Peter, "Feed my sheep."

Even before I had finished my remarks, I knew that they were not being well received by everyone. I had clearly heard a couple of disapproving grunts from one of my colleagues whose field was ethics, but who took an intense though uninformed interest in matters liturgical. Afterwards, when the meeting merged into a social gathering, I got the indictment that I sensed was coming. I overheard the ethicist telling another faculty member, and it was clear that he wanted me to hear, "The trouble with May is he thinks everything has to have meaning."

It is a comment that has stayed with me, not, I must confess, because it offended me the way Ruby Turpin was in Flannery O'Connor's story "Revelation," by Mary Grace's telling her, "Go back to hell where you came from, you old wart hog." It did not really hurt at all, actually, except to emphasize for me the chasm that I knew divided me from the theological sensibility of my colleague and many like him. I remember, in fact, getting a kind of perverse enjoyment from the remark and being immediately anxious to leave the gathering to tell the story to some friends who shared my sense of relief at the reforms of the council. What the ethicist said was true, but the problem latent in his judgment was not mine alone. It was *ours* because there seemed at the time to be no way to bring our diverging views of the world of faith together.

On many occasions since then, when I have recounted the story, I have always added that I would like to have offered my colleague an important distinction, one that was as true for me then as it is now—a distinction I hope would have made my colleague think a bit more kindly of me. That everything pertaining to faith has to have meaning that is intelligible to us at all times would of course be sheer folly and utter pride. That it has meaning that needs always to be sought, even if that meaning is never adequately uncovered, seems to me to be a necessary consequence of belief in a God of revelation.

Then, as now, I am convinced that my colleague feared that, in the spirit of certain so-called "liberal Protestant" approaches to the faith popular at the time (needless to say Bultmann's existentialist kerygma was viewed with suspicion if not horror at the college), I was prepared to throw out any article of faith that was not immediately relevant to the contemporary mind. To the best of my recollection, that was never true. I was nonetheless fully aware that my eucharistic analogy had been intentionally forceful, if not tactless.

That was 1965, and it is fair to say that, at the time, the custodians of traditional theology were less than comfortable with the idea of "meaning." Today, meaning is still under fire but, by a curious twist of fate, from my perspective at least, it is under fire from the "left" rather than from the "right," from the self-styled heralds of our literary future, critics that John Updike has labeled "connoisseurs of textual self-betrayal"—namely, the champions of deconstruction and other abstruse postmodern critical theories. At the turn of the millennium, I find myself in a fairly typical department of English—at least for a large state university—with its representative share of avant-garde theorists. We have our regular meetings too, but very few of them, frankly, are as cordial as the ones I remember from the 1960s. And although one almost never overhears comments in public before, during, or after the meetings, one occasionally hears via the grapevine what is said in the privacy of certain offices. Rumor has it that some of my colleagues are offering, in private, a variation on the tongues of old: "The problem with May," the report goes, "is that he thinks texts have meaning." The purpose of the critic, these colleagues insist, is to deconstruct texts to show how they subvert the very meaning they seem to be conveying. Put another way, your opinion of what the text is about is as good as mine. My contemporary colleagues, like the traditionalists of old, do not openly contest my views. Rather, the cautious tolerance of both groups has preferred to leave me in my ignorance—yesteryear because of charity, today because of an enlightened sense of pluralism. The more things change, the French proverb goes, the more they remain the same.

Now I have little hope of ever reconciling my views about the literary text with the disciples of deconstruction; my only consolation lies in the personal conviction that the current literary critical "orthodoxies" are fads that will take their toll on our students for a while then vanish. I am devoted to the conviction that artists want to communicate with their audiences and, thus, texts, of necessity, must have meaning that can be discerned, however sketchily. The novelist Walker Percy was, in my opinion, one hundred percent correct when, in an essay on Herman Melville, he commented on the matter of artistic communication: "Lonely as is the craft of writing, it is the most social of vocations. No matter what the writer may say, the work is always written to someone, for someone, against someone."

In the realm of theology, though, I have always had the hope of reconciliation. The truth of the matter is that traditional Christian theology provided its own distinction to bridge the apparent chasm that was separating me from the ethicist. For each mystery of faith, it directed us to distinguish between its meaning in itself (*in se*) and its meaning for us (*quoad nos*). For example, in treating God's creation of the world, traditional theology approached the mystery *in itself* in terms of the concept of creation "out of nothing" and its consequences *for us* through an explanation of creaturehood, radical dependence, and stewardship. The less accessible mysteries of our faith, the mysteries strictly so-called of the Trinity and the Incarnation, can never be wholly intelligible to us *in themselves*. Even our ability to understand some of the more accessible mysteries waxes and wanes. But that does not mean, as I suggested my colleague from the 1960s feared, that I feel that such mysteries are, therefore, no longer integral to our faith. The Church's task is precisely to discover the language that will expose each mystery *in itself*, even if only partially, to the light of contemporary understanding. Efforts to elucidate the meaning *for our lives*, even of belief in the Incarnation and the Trinity, is never as difficult.

The explanation of the meaning of the mysteries *in themselves*, insofar as that is possible, is the work of theologians. Our task as ordinary believers is to discover, with the help of theologians, what the implications of those mysteries are *for us*—their meaning for our daily lives of faith. Anyone who has struggled to live the Christian faith maturely knows that meaning *for us* is not a given of our lives either. It must be sought, discovered, nurtured, shared. We are too often content with the mere verbal profession of the articles of the creed without having any clear idea of why it is so important for us to profess them (meaning *for us*), much less what it is that we are actually professing to believe (meaning *in itself*).

My experience of shifting worlds aside, this work would not have been possible for me if I had not had in the late '60s the opportunity to pursue graduate studies in theology and literature. Before that, I had an instinctive feeling that the literature that I had read with enthusiasm for as long as I could remember and the great films that I had seen had had a strong influence on my life and my faith. What further studies provided, of course, was a solid understanding of the reasons for the essential bond that unites literature and film with belief. It was the suspicion that such a relationship existed that had led me to select theology and literature as my field of specialization. Since then, two of the constants of my life, my love of literature and film and my commitment to Christianity, have been consciously united in a profoundly gratifying way.

Thus, what I had intuitively sensed, I came to know through conscious reflection to be unquestionably true: literature and film had just as surely contributed to the growth of my faith as theology itself and perhaps more, precisely because literature and film reach the *whole* person, whereas the reasoned discourse of theology appeals primarily to the mind. The fact that stories appeal to the whole person is no doubt one of the reasons Jesus used parables to instill a feeling for the new order of God's kingdom that he was instituting.

That Jesus taught in parables is evident from the Gospels themselves; that many of his parables are stories in the strict sense needs perhaps some explanation. Biblical scholars usually distinguish four types of parables: comparisons, examples, allegories, and stories. The comparisons (e.g., the lost coin, the pearl merchant) present a familiar image, a typical recurring scene from everyday life, and thus have their effect by appealing to what is universally understood; the examples (e.g., the good Samaritan, the Pharisee and the publican) tell us exactly what we should do or avoid. Allegories describe our relationship with the intangible world by assigning transcendent values—God, spiritual attributes and powers, virtues or vices—to concrete elements of the story, or by creating characters who clearly represent these realities. The perfect example of a gospel allegory, and the only parable explicitly interpreted as an allegory by the synoptic evangelists, is the parable of the sower and the seed. Many scholars feel that the parable of the pounds in Luke 19:12–27 is also an allegory.

The parables that are stories in the strict sense, though, are freely invented, dramatic narratives involving conflicts between human beings that symbolize or suggest rather than explicitly describe our relationship with God. In the everyday language of a classical literary distinction, they *show* us rather than *tell* us. The great wedding feast, the prodigal son, the talents, the ten maidens, the unforgiving servant, the unjust steward, the wedding garment, the wicked tenants, and the workers in the vineyard fall into this last category of parables. They provide us with instances of Jesus' storytelling art and prove, as it were, that stories themselves can be bearers of religious meaning, even if they affect us only indirectly, figuratively, imaginatively. Indeed, they possess the kind of ambiguity that we have come to associate with all art. The extreme effect of this ambiguity is expressed in Mark 4:11–12, where the evangelist states that Jesus taught in parables purposely to conceal the truth from those destined to remain in their sins. It is no distortion of his words, I feel, to reexpress them this way: the hardened of heart will not be predisposed to understand. Jesus invariably praised those who were open to belief. Moreover, it is difficult to believe that Jesus would have told stories if they were incapable of being understood at least in some sense.

Like all stories, too, Jesus' parables affect the whole person. And what affects the whole person does so below the level of awareness, another reason why stories have such power over us, and why we ought not to read just any book or see movies indiscriminately. There is an extraordinary passage in T. S. Eliot's classic essay on "Religion and Literature" that speaks with clarity and precision about the power of literature (the same obviously can be said of film):

> If we, as readers, keep our religious and moral convictions in a compartment, and take our reading merely for entertainment, or on a higher plane, for aesthetic pleasure, I would point out that the author, whatever his conscious intentions in writing, in practice recognizes no such distinctions. The author of a work of imagination is trying to affect us wholly, as human beings, whether he knows it or not; and we are affected by it, as human beings, whether we intend to be or not. I suppose that everything we eat has some other effect upon us than merely the pleasure of taste and mastication; it affects us during the process of assimilation and digestion; and I believe that exactly the same is true of anything we read (from *Essays Ancient and Modern*).

The power of film to affect us has been described more recently, but just as forcefully by the critic Roger Angell:

> Movies are felt by the audience long before they are "understood." Going to the movies, in fact, is not an intellectual process most of the time but an emotional one. Any serious, well-made movie we see seems to wash over us there in the dark, bathing us in feelings and suggestions, and imparting a deep or light tinge of meaning that stays with us, sometimes for life.

Frank Capra, one of the truly great directors of cinema's first century, left us in his autobiography—*Frank Capra: The Name Above the Title*—this testimony from the artist's viewpoint to the consequences of film's power: "Only the morally courageous are worthy of speaking to their fellow men for two hours in the dark. And only the artistically incorrupt will earn and keep the people's trust." This quotation is particularly close to the heart of my purpose in writing this book—namely, our need to discern for ourselves or to be directed by others to the literature and films of the "morally courageous" and the "artistically incorrupt." These are the fictions that will be supportive of faith.

Faith, as much if not more than any other significant aspect of our lives, must be nurtured or it will, for all practical purposes, wither and die. The books that we read and the films that we see will affect our vision of the world just as surely as breathing and eating enable us to live. It stands to reason, therefore, that we ought to make literature and film work for the growth of faith, and they will if they portray a vision of life and its meaning—if they create a fictional world—that is compatible with the worldview that our faith directs us to acknowledge. To put it more positively, we will most surely nurture our faith by reading literature and viewing films that are sensitive to the faith we profess to the extent that they deepen our awareness of faith's meaning *for us*.

A novelist and short-story writer whose works have had a profound influence on my appreciation of Christianity is the southern, Catholic fiction writer Flannery O'Connor, whose extraordinary story "Revelation" I have already referred to. A letter that she wrote to a student at Emory University sheds light on our discussion precisely because it addresses the notion of cultivating faith through reading. Alfred Corn had heard O'Connor give a talk and then, too shy to approach her personally, had written her afterwards because he was impressed by the quality of her faith—at a time when he felt he was losing his own. Her letter, dated May 30, 1962, two years before her death, urges him to read, read, read. "If you want your faith, you have to work for it. It is a gift, but for very few is it a gift given without any demand for equal time devoted to its cultivation," she wrote—and the latter comment I obviously find myself in complete accord with. "For every book you read that is anti-Christian," she went on, "make it your business to read one that presents the other side of the picture; if one isn't satisfactory to you, read others." Having recommended that he read Pierre Teilhard de Chardin, Etienne Gilson, and Cardinal Newman, she explained: "To find out about faith, you have to go to the people who have it and you have to go to the most intelligent ones." She nonetheless cautioned him that more than intellect was involved, using Gerard Manley Hopkins's advice to Robert Bridges, "Give alms," as evidence of the need for nourishing faith through good deeds, and thus for finding faith through love, of experiencing God in other human beings. Insight of this sort, I would add, can just as easily be gained from a story as from reasoned discourse.

In the late 1970s, I was invited by the Catholic Center at Louisiana State University to speak in its annual "Last Lecture Series." "What would you say," the question was put to me, "if you were to face an audience for one last time?" It was an excellent conceit for a lecture series, and I was deeply honored to have been asked to speak. My thesis, with more than a passing act of gratitude to Flannery O'Connor, was simply this: "We become what we read." As I look back today at my notes for that lecture of two decades ago, I am pleased to notice that I gave balanced recognition to Teilhard de Chardin and the *Epic of Gilgamesh*, Erick Erickson and Dante, Dietrich Bonhoeffer and Flannery O'Connor. It was almost, as I reflect now, a dress rehearsal for this book.

The fictional dimension of this work I approach primarily as an enthusiastic reader and an avid moviegoer. From what I have already said, it should be clear that I view art, and thus fiction, as communication, and so believe that our task as readers and viewers is to submit ourselves to the whole work before us in the hopes that we can come as close as possible to grasping the artist's meaning. The "fiction" of my title is, of course, the general term I use for "freely invented stories of the artistic imagination," a term, therefore, that includes both literature and film. Among literary texts, I will appeal to novels, short stories, and plays; the films are limited exclusively to so-called "feature films."

As a critic, I respect what is called the *autonomy* of both literature and film; namely, that literary and cinematic texts must be approached on their own terms and not have categories imposed upon them. Practically speaking, I try not to find theological language where there is none or to search out isolated religious elements in literature and film as if these were the most important indicators of meaning in fiction. Rather, I think that we must strive to allow the concrete *wholeness* of the work to have its effect on our interpretation, to come to some overall sense of the "world of the work"—because that is what affects us "wholly, as human beings," in Eliot's words, and thus has the potential to nourish faith.

Limits of space prohibit lengthy analyses of the works I refer to; in many instances, individual lines and particular scenes will be the focus of my attention, but only, I insist, as reflectors of the whole work. There will also be a few occasions where I refer to works that, as a whole, do not support a Christian view of the world—and I make this clear in the text—but that offer isolated images or insights that can be helpful to the believer.

In the final analysis, respect for autonomy of the text aside, literature and film as types of fiction will be considered here only insofar as they have been judged to be the handmaidens of faith. Clearly not all works of fiction are conducive to the nourishment of faith; some are, in fact, positively harmful. Our perennial task as believers is one of cultural discernment, and since most stories today, like the parables of Jesus, will not have any explicit religious references at all, the literary or cinematic work's Christian dimension must be sought in terms of its everyday human analogue.

The dimensions of "faith," as I understand it here, also need some clarification. Faith is often and, I think, appropriately described, as a personal commitment to God's initiative of salvation revealed in Jesus Christ and sustained today by their life-giving Spirit. Our most solemn professions of this commitment are found, of course, in the creeds of Christianity, and of those creeds, the oldest and most venerable is the Apostles' Creed. It is also the most universally accepted creed within the Christian churches and hence the most ecumenical—added reasons why I have chosen it as the evidence for those fundamental truths of our faith that we need constantly to be seeking the meaning of for our daily lives (*quoad nos*).

The version of the Apostles' Creed that we use today has been basically unchanged in the West since the time of Charlemagne (c. A.D. 800). With the exception of four phrases—*creator of heaven and earth, he descended into hell, the communion of saints*, and *life everlasting*—it is basically the same creed that Rufinus of Aquileia, around the year A.D. 404, calls the Roman Creed and that scholars believe must date in creedal form from very early in the third century because of its striking similarity to the baptismal profession of faith given in Hippolytus's *Apostolic Tradition* (c. A.D. 217). Rufinus attributes the creed to the apostles and tells the story of its composition by the twelve assembled together, with each contributing one of its propositions. Whereas one can safely consider that a pious legend at best, it has been the venerable tradition of the Church that the substance of the creed is clearly of apostolic origin.

Although later and fuller versions of the creed, like the Nicene or Athanasian Creeds, include phrases and clauses that grew out of the resolution of specific theological controversies, the earliest creeds do not seem to have been formulated in response to errors about the faith. Rather, they developed apparently in the radically affirmative catechetical and liturgical setting of the reception of new believers into the full communion of the Church. Thus, our earliest creedal texts, like the creed of Hippolytus, are in the interrogative form of the baptismal confession. Converts signify their faith in the Triune God, then, as they do now, by their responses to the questions of the minister of the sacrament of baptism.

There is perhaps no more vivid representation in fiction of what the total commitment of faith ultimately involves than Robert Bolt's play *A Man for All Seasons*, adapted for the screen by Fred Zinnemann. The man for all seasons is Sir Thomas More, Chancellor of England, who was beheaded for his refusal to take the oath of allegiance to King Henry VIII, that effectively denied the primal authority of the pope within the Church. Even though Robert Bolt admits that he does not share More's belief, he is obviously fascinated by the personal strength of the figure who dominates his play. The heroic sense of self that More's gift of faith instilled in him is surely as satisfactory an explanation as can be found for his willingness to die for his belief. In the introduction to the published play, Bolt writes eloquently about More's sense of self:

> He knew where he began and left off, what area of himself he could yield to the encroachments of his enemies, and what to the encroachments of those he loved. It was a substantial area in both cases, for he had a proper sense of fear and was a busy lover. Since he was a clever man and a great lawyer he was able to retire from those areas in wonderfully good order, but at length he was asked to retreat from that final area where he located his self. And there this supple, humorous, unassuming and sophisticated person set like metal, was overtaken by an absolutely primitive rigor, and could no more be budged than a cliff.

The dialogue of the play speaks even more eloquently to the subject of a self informed by faith when the Duke of Norfolk tries to persuade More to give in to the king's demands:

> *Norfolk:* Does this make sense? . . . You'll forfeit all you've got—which includes the respect of your country—for a theory?
> *More:* The Apostolic Succession of the Pope is— . . . Why, it's a theory, yes; you can't see it; can't touch it; it's a theory. . . . But what matters to me is not whether it's true or not but that I believe it to be true, or rather, not that I *believe* it, but that *I* believe it.

Later, More uses the English nobility's current craze for water spaniels as a way of explaining the logic of his position:

> *More:* The nobility of England, my lord, would have snored through the Sermon on the Mount. But you'll labor like Thomas Aquinas over a rat-dog's pedigree. Now what's the name of those distorted creatures you're all breeding at the moment? . . .
> *Norfolk:* Water spaniels!
> *More:* And what would you do with a water spaniel that was afraid of water? You'd hang it! Well, as a spaniel is to water, so is a man to

his own self. I will not give in because I oppose it—I do—not my pride, not my spleen, nor any other of my appetites but *I do—I!*

Only when More, imprisoned in the tower, is challenged by his daughter, Margaret, does he explain fully, but simply, the basis of his decision:

Margaret: But in reason! Haven't you done as much as God can reasonably *want*?
More: Well . . . finally . . . it isn't a matter of reason; finally it's a matter of love.

With More's confession, we have touched upon the heart of the mystery of our redemption and, indeed, upon the heart of the mystery of faith's commitment. We have also to a certain extent gotten ahead of our demonstration of fiction's capacity to nourish our faith. Saint Thomas More presents us with an image of the ultimate demand that faith can make on us in terms of commitment, and even if the ordinary way of faith is not the way of martyrdom—the day-to-day quality of our commitment, in fact, is more often distracted and faltering, even at times confused—it never hurts to keep the ideal clearly before us; namely, that genuine commitment is not finally a matter of knowledge, but of love.

To conclude these introductory observations, the twofold purpose of this book, in brief, is to share an understanding of the meaning of the fundamental truths of the Christian faith *for us* as well as insights into fiction's capacity to serve the growth of that faith. In personal terms, I wish to give testimony to both my perception of the meaning of the Apostles' Creed for our lives and my appreciation of the Christian dimensions of literature and film. My witness, of course, is necessarily limited, on one hand, by my own reflections on our faith's meaning for our lives—although here I have been aided significantly by the theologians I have read—and, on the other hand, by my personal literary and cinematic preferences, which have more often than not been informed by my Catholic education and experience as a teacher. Readers may therefore legitimately wonder why some films and works of literature are mentioned and others are not—an excellent sign that the virus has spread, and that so-called "secular" texts are being judged by others as not so secular after all. My only response can be that the works of literary and cinematic imagination recommended here are, as a matter of fact, the ones that helped me in a special way to deepen my insight into the meaning of the Apostles' Creed for my life, and that I have in some instances returned to over and over again to enrich my life as a Catholic.

Aside from this Introduction and the brief Conclusion, the three divisions of the book seek to preserve in their titles a sense of our Triune confession of faith by appealing to the persons of the Trinity, according to their attributed roles in the economy of salvation: "Stories of the Creator," "Stories of the Savior," and "Stories of the Lifegiver." "Story" is the comprehensive term that fits the narrative foundation of both literature and film even if for the sake of irony—and alliteration—I have used "fiction" alone in the title to cover both literature and film. For fictional analogues to our belief in the persons of the Trinity, use of the terms *Creator* and *Savior* need little explanation—*Creator* as the fundamental activity of the Father is found in the Apostles' Creed, and even though the word *Savior* as such is not, the story of our salvation is clearly narrated in the second part of the creed. *Lifegiver* as a title for the Holy Spirit comes from the fuller Nicene Creed, the eucharistic community's profession of faith. There we proclaim the Holy Spirit as both "Lord" and "giver of life." Calling the Spirit Lord, "the name that is above every name," is of course the creed's way of noting the equality of persons in the Trinity. "Giver of life," on the other hand, is the Nicene Creed's special title for the Third Person of the Trinity—hence my reason for choosing "Stories of the Lifegiver" as appropriate for fictional analogues to the work of the Holy Spirit in salvation history.

Huston Smith, in *The Religions of Man,* says that all the major world religions strive to answer three fundamental questions: Is the universe experienced as benign, indifferent, or malignant? Is salvation a matter of the head or the heart? Is it gained alone or with others? These are, as a matter of fact, the basic questions that the three parts of the book will seek in succession to explore fictional responses to—visions of the world in novels, plays, short stories, and movies that correspond to Christianity's distinctive answers in the worldview of the Apostles' Creed.

Like the other major religions, Christianity claims to give us a sense of ourselves and of our proper relationship with other human beings, with the world that surrounds us, and with a reality that transcends our senses and often eludes our awareness—ultimate reality. Unlike the Eastern religions, though, the religions of the West—Judaism, Christianity, and Islam—discover their visions of the world in the one God's unique revelation in history. And, of course, among the Western religions, Christianity alone believes that there is no satisfying answer to life's questions or appropriate response to its challenges apart from the life, death, and resurrection of God's only Son, Jesus Christ, and their lifegiving Spirit.

At the heart of the Christian experience is the unavoidable and joyous admission that we are living in a new age, not so radically new that the roots of its newness are not found in the longings of earlier religious communities, especially Judaism, but radically new just the same in a wonderful, provocative, and grace-filled way. The uniqueness of this vision of the world and of the consequent purpose of our lives that God has revealed to us in Jesus will become clearer, I hope, as we discover its reflection in some of the great works of literary and cinematic imagination in our time. In the West, the Bible has been the single most influential text; it is, in fact, so much a part of our American Jewish-Christian cultural roots that its stories, images, and symbols continue to influence the imagination of artists whether they are believers or not.

Although the emphasis in each of the three parts of this work will be, as I have indicated, on correspondences to the Trinitarian sense of world that unfolds in the Apostles' Creed, I have nonetheless made an effort to reflect upon the individual articles of the creed where they can readily be discerned in fiction, a project that was clearly easier in the first and third parts of the book than in the second. Attempts to find cultural correlations to all of the mysteries accompanying the passion, death, and resurrection of Jesus—the union of human and divine natures in Christ, Mary's conception by the Holy Spirit, the virgin birth, the descent into hell, and ascent into heaven—more often than not seem either artificial or forced. Some commentators, for example, consider so-called "buddy stories," involving unevenly talented main characters like *Of Mice and Men* and *Rain Man,* as reflections of the two natures in Christ. However, inasmuch as my professed preference is for emphasizing the literary or cinematic work's overall "sense of world" or, as Eliseo Vivas puts it simply, "the world of the work," I wanted to avoid, as much as possible, the appearance of reading meanings *into* texts. Hence, I have chosen in Part Two, as I explain there, to focus on "stories of the Savior" that deal with the heart of the mystery of our redemption. To facilitate transitions within the text, I have provided headings that I hope will be helpful to my readers, as well as an Appendix that offers an outline of the interior divisions of the book, highlighting the works treated in detail and others both briefly noted and recommended.

In the final analysis, I will feel that I have achieved my purpose if I have shown to my readers' satisfaction how literature and film can contribute to the growth of our Christian faith. I hope to show the folly, as well, of thinking that "secular" culture is devoid of religious significance. Although I have written this book with the committed believer in mind, I nonetheless hope that others may find it helpful. Perhaps, for those who doubt, it may occasion some rebirth of insight that will yield a new day of belief. For those who do not profess the same faith, I hope that this exposition helps demonstrate the support for mature, purposeful living that can be found in the best literature and cinema of our culture, so permeated as it is with the rich images and ennobling values of our Jewish-Christian heritage.

I believe in God, the Father almighty,
creator of heaven and earth.

A thought, a material improvement, a harmony, a particular expression of love, the enchanting complexity of a smile or a look, all the new beauties that appear for the first time, in me or around me, on the human face of the earth—I cherish them like children and cannot believe that they will die entirely in the flesh. If I believed that these things were to wither away for ever, should I have given them life? The more I examine myself, the more I discover this psychological truth: that no one lifts his little finger to do the smallest task unless moved, however obscurely, by the conviction that he is contributing infinitesimally (at least indirectly) to the construction of some absolute—that is to say, to Your work, my God. . . . Show all Your faithful, Lord, in what a full and true sense "their work follows them" into Your Kingdom. . . . Otherwise they will become like those idle laborers who are not spurred by their task; . . . and it will be said that the sons of heaven cannot compete on the human level, in conviction and hence on equal terms, with the children of the world.

—Pierre Teilhard de Chardin, *The Divine Milieu*

I
STORIES OF THE CREATOR

There is a deeply affecting moment at the center of Tennessee Williams's *A Streetcar Named Desire* that many consider to represent the greatest affirmation in all of his plays. Those who have not seen the play have perhaps had the pleasure of viewing Elia Kazan's classic film adaptation, starring Vivien Leigh, Marlon Brando, and Karl Malden. There is so much that is memorable about the film, but nothing that quite touches the poetry of this crucial scene that ends in a startling revelation, if not a profession of faith. Blanche DuBois, whose name itself suggests the world of illusion she has been trapped in, is invited out for the evening by Mitch, a middle-aged bachelor and a friend of her brother-in-law Stanley Kowalski. Mitch is a mother's boy who needs a genuine romantic relationship; Blanche wants someone to redeem her from her shameful past by loving her true, inner beauty. As the evening draws on, the two begin to realize that they have something in common. Mitch says simply, "You need somebody, and I need somebody, too. Could it be—you and me, Blanche?" And she exclaims, near ecstasy, "Sometimes—there's God—so quickly." It is a touching portrayal of the sanctity of interpersonal relations as well as a declaration of a way in which God can indeed be experienced.

As a matter of fact, one of the twentieth century's genuinely satisfying philosophical demonstrations of God's existence places our experience of the divine precisely in the sacredness of that encounter between persons. Our benefactor is Martin Buber, Jewish philosopher and theologian, and the name of his major work is *I and Thou*. No longer, Buber writes, do those who seek evidence of God's existence look to rational arguments, whether based on our sense of the universe's order, purpose, beauty, contingency, or origin, as St. Thomas Aquinas centuries before attempted to do. Rather, God is to be experienced, Buber explains, by the whole person in the mystery of the revelation of the self to another, of an "I" to any "Thou." That moment of the meeting and total sharing between persons is mysterious, sacred, indeed divine because only the presence of God can account for the dissolution of the protective shield we hide ourselves within—which alone makes personal encounter possible. Whether or not we agree with Buber about the usefulness today of St. Thomas's proofs for the existence of God—many of course continue to find them quite helpful—we can surely profit also from Martin Buber's extraordinary insight into our experience of God in the genuine encounter of persons.

God the Caring Father: Personal Sense of Belonging

Although *A Streetcar Named Desire*, taken in its entirety, cannot reasonably be considered a story of the Creator, because it does more than suggest that the world is at best indifferent to our fate, if not positively malignant, we do not have to go far—in fact, only to two other Southern writers—to find works that provide a view of the world in which the experience of belonging or of being cared for is analogous to faith's confession of a loving Father. Moreover, as we will discover, it is often the case with literature and film that artists will present us with an affirmation about life that is discovered in the depiction of its opposite. Flannery O'Connor's story "The River" is, among other things, about the hunger for belonging that every human being experiences. The same concern is at the heart of Carson McCullers's novel *The Member of the Wedding* and Fred Zinnemann's movie of the same name, adapted for the screen from McCullers's own dramatization of her novel for the stage.

Typically, O'Connor's representation in "The River" of the theme of belonging is bizarre and indirect. Harry Ashfield, a young child growing up in an urban setting, has parents more interested in their own self-indulgence than they are in caring for him. On Sundays, they regularly commit him to the care of a country woman so that they can sleep off their hangovers from the night before. The name Ashfield itself, suggesting the perpetual disarray of their apartment following their revelries, is a reminder of the barren atmosphere the child is subjected to.

Mrs. Connin, Harry's keeper for the day, is one of O'Connor's outspoken believers. The first clear image we have of her as she looms in the doorway of the Ashfields' apartment is of "a speckled skeleton, in a long pea-green coat and felt helmet," and we sense immediately the presence of death. When the image of the skeleton is associated with her once again, later in the story, we know enough about her determined faith to be sure that the death she foreshadows is a passage into life. Mrs. Connin, like all of O'Connor's fundamentalist believers, puts Harry—and us—in contact with God. Her plan for the day, an intention she announces bluntly to Harry's father, is to take Harry to the river for a healing. The Reverend Bevel Summers, a preacher only occasionally in those parts, will be praying over the sick, and Mrs. Connin naively suggests that the ailing Mrs. Ashfield herself "ought to see him sometime."

At the river Harry, who perversely insists that his first name is the same as the preacher's, listens intently to the Reverend Summers talk about "the River of Life, made out of Jesus' Blood." And when Mrs. Connin tells the preacher that she suspects the little boy has not been baptized, the preacher instructs her to "swang him over here," and he promises Harry-Bevel that he will never be the same if he is received by "the deep river of life." "You'll count," the preacher says, and that is an experience Harry knows he has never had at home. But he is too young to understand the meaning of the symbols the preacher uses; his preliterate mind equates symbol and reality. Back at home, he is grilled by his parents, who are furious at the presumption of Mrs. Connin and the Reverend Summers in baptizing him. His name, they clarify for Mrs. Connin's sake, is Harry not Bevel. His mother questions him in bed about what the preacher said, pulling Harry to a sitting position, and the child has the uncomfortable feeling "as if he had been drawn up from under the water," a clear reminder to us that at home he does not count. The child simply mutters, "He said I'm not the same now. . . . I count."

Naming goes with baptism—the name symbolic of the new life of the baptized. Harry *is* Bevel because there is a place identified by his namesake as the River of Life where he does count. The tragic irony of the story, which we know in O'Connor's perspective is more of a *felix culpa* than a real tragedy, is that Bevel goes back to the river to be received by it completely, and there accidentally drowns. Yet, short of our needing to supply faith's vision of the child being received into the fullness of God's kingdom, the story helps us to understand through its various levels of contrast—belief and disbelief, country and city, simplicity and sophistication—that there is, indeed, a world in which each of us counts and that world is the community of faith in a caring Father.

Just as surely as the explicit religious language is part of O'Connor's story, it is absent from McCullers's tale; but that does not detract a bit from the shared thematic material of these two Georgia writers—the need to belong. O'Connor's short story reveals in the extremes mentioned above the difference between "counting" and "not counting"; Carson McCullers's novel, turned play and film, traces the development of a sense of belonging in its young heroine. "The River" focuses on the needs of an all-but-abandoned five-year-old boy; *The Member of the Wedding*, on the freakish antics of a motherless, twelve-year-old tomboy. Changes of name are central to both stories. Harry Ashfield's taking of the name Bevel shows his unconscious preference for a world of belonging; Frankie Addams, who considers herself "a member of nothing in the world," assumes the name F. Jasmine when she is asked to be "a member of the wedding" of her brother Jarvis to Janice Williams. She wants her name to begin with the same letter as theirs, and to be similar in sound and syllable.

Although Frankie grows into accepting her own given name, which is Frances, it is clear from the title of the novel and from her sense of belonging when asked to be in her brother's wedding that her use of the name F. Jasmine is indeed a rite of passage to a more mature sense of self in the midst of others. The invitation is her introduction to a sense of belonging; of her brother and his wife to be, she comes to think, "They are the we of me." There is a poetic simplicity to this statement, a pubescent girl's ebullient celebration of belonging. It is clearly the most memorable line from the novel, and one that has been immortalized along with the character of Frankie-Frances by Julie Harris's performance of that role in Fred Zinnemann's film *The Member of the Wedding*.

Harris was twenty-six when the film was shot, yet her transformation into an awkward, but irrepressible twelve-year-old is a masterpiece of film acting. What the film shows so tenderly, however, and the novel only suggests, is that Frankie was mistaken about her "we." That Bernice, the maid, and John Henry, her young friend, are her true "we" is obvious from the medium-close three-shot that becomes finally a close-close-up simply of their heads nestled together. Zinnemann uses this composition of frame to show their intimacy as they sing the hymn, "For Jesus is my portion, /My constant companion is He, /For His eye is on the sparrow, /And I know he watches me."

Cosmic Sense of Belonging

A number of other films that are potent stories of the Creator place our sense of belonging in a more humbling, cosmic context. Among the most notable are John Ford's *Stagecoach*, Federico Fellini's *La Strada*, and Lawrence Kasdan's *Grand Canyon*. *Stagecoach* is one of John Ford's greatest films and, for some, still the best western ever made. The son of Irish immigrants, Ford never abandoned his strong sense of human interdependence and finitude. Even though he expects tolerance of everyone as the minimum virtue for belonging to the human family, his film suggests that only those who think of others ahead of themselves can provide a confident basis for lasting community. Nevertheless, it is the repeated establishing shots against the majestic background of Monument Valley that we remember the most, a symbolic reminder of the pettiness of our human pretensions in view of life's grand design and our radical dependence upon God.

La Strada ("the road")—an ideal image for life's pilgrimage—tells the story of a traveling stuntman, Zampano, who pays a country woman ten thousand lire for the services of her daughter Gelsomina. Zampano is crude, even mean; Gelsomina, a simpleminded but devoted young woman (played to perfection by Fellini's wife, Giulietta Masina), whose face itself is a universe of expression. The harder Gelsomina tries to help Zampano stage his roadside act—breaking a chain around his chest with his muscles—the more insensitive he becomes. In Rome they meet up with a circus troupe, and one of the performers, ironically called the Fool, answers the despairing Gelsomina's question, "Oh, why was I born?" by saying, "If *you* didn't stay with [Zampano], who would? Everything in this world is good for . . . for something." Then the Fool picks up a stone, telling her that even it has a purpose. "What's it good for?" she snaps, and he responds, "If I knew that, I would be God. But if this stone is useless, then everything is, even the stars. You, too . . . you have a purpose too." The Fool's stone is a microcosm of meaning, but the sea and the stars provide the film's final cosmic context of belonging. Throughout, Gelsomina is associated with the sea, so that at the end when Zampano, who has just heard the news of her untimely death, falls to his knees on the seashore at night and weeps, we are meant to understand that Gelsomina is present and that Zampano has a rare moment of insight into the purpose of all things—and persons— great *and* small.

Lawrence Kasdan's *Grand Canyon* is, to my mind, a truly powerful and meaningful film; it is certainly one of the most explicitly religious American films of the 1990s. I attribute this in large part to the intelligent script by Kasdan and his wife, Meg, who together won the film's only Academy Award, for best original screenplay. The title itself announces the film's symbol for cosmic purpose, its conviction that there is a design that overrides the chaos of contemporary urban society and that will surely survive it the way the beauty of the Grand Canyon has transcended the geological ravages of eons. Even though there are dimensions of the film that, I hope to show later, can also nourish our faith in the Holy Spirit as Lifegiver, it deserves screening as a story of the Creator.

Released about a half a year before the April 1992 riots in South Central Los Angeles, it seems eerily prophetic of those events when viewed now, even though it is not directly concerned with racial and ethnic tensions. The police helicopters that dart ominously across the nighttime sky over L.A.'s inner urban canyon of unrest are a reminder of impending disaster, but also a refrain for the kind of detached surveillance of chaos that ultimately achieves little, except perhaps the rescue of the dead and dying. They are as effective, one critic has pointed out, as the omnipresent helicopters in movies about Vietnam that have come to be associated with our failed efforts there.

These observations may make the film seem needlessly negative, if not despairing. Indeed there are intense, though brief, outbursts of violence and incidences of natural tragedy in the film: the threat of death from an inner-city gang, a robber in broad daylight shooting for a watch, a baby girl abandoned in a suburban cove, the home of a black family riddled by the firing of a machine gun, a heart attack during an earthquake, to mention the most striking. But, in the words of Davis, the film's producer of ultraviolent B-movies about urban "rage," these instances are simply "realistic" evidence of contemporary urban life. Each is also in the worldview of the film dramatically crucial to the bonding of the characters.

In its opening sequence, *Grand Canyon* sets up the relationship that makes it finally such a powerful story of the Creator. Mack, a white immigration lawyer whose sensibilities are middle-class liberal, is saved from almost certain death when he runs out of gas in a black ghetto trying to avoid a traffic jam following a Lakers game. His savior is Simon, a black tow-truck operator, responding to his call, who smoothly talks the black gang out of a fight that they may, he warns, live to regret. The bond that develops between the two men unifies the film. Simon tells Mack, who has never been to the Grand Canyon, what its significance is for him in these words: "The thing that got me was sitting on the edge of that big old thing . . . those rocks and those cliffs . . . they're so old. . . . And one of us? That's a piece of time too small to give a name. . . . Those rocks are laughing at me, I can tell. Me and my worries." If Simon's reflections on the Grand Canyon seem somewhat stoical and deterministic, this is surely to be understood, if not forgiven, by reason of the obstacles he has had to overcome simply to live. In the context of the whole film, it is abundantly clear that his reflection is one of both wonder and humility, a foreshadowing of his wisdom later on in inviting his friend to take some time out from life's hectic pace and often tragic patterns to rest, and to contemplate one of nature's singularly awe-inspiring sights.

Stories of the Creator, therefore, offer responses to the first fundamental question that Huston Smith says all religions answer—namely, how do we experience the world? Is it benign, indifferent, or malignant? Specifically, stories of the Creator give us a sense of belonging in the world, of being at ease in our surroundings, that corresponds to our experience in faith of a world that is benevolently conceived and providentially designed, because it is the work of our heavenly Father.

The first article of the Apostles' Creed acknowledges our new and most unique personal relationship with ultimate reality; namely, with God as Father—a relationship different even from that of our spiritual ancestors, the Jews. Our confident confession of God as Father, therefore, is initially the most unique feature of our creed; it sets the tone for our vision of reality. For, as Christianity emerged from Judaism and began to shape its creed, the God of our Fathers—of Abraham, Isaac, and Jacob—became the Father of each and every individual, one who knows no distinctions of race or nation, of status in society, or of gender: "There is no such thing as Jew and Greek, slave and freeman, male and female" (Galatians 3:28). When Jesus' disciples asked him how they should pray, he told them to begin by saying, "Our father." Up until the time of Jesus, Jews addressed God in a variety of ways; they proclaimed him the Father of Israel, their nation (see Deuteronomy 32:6; Jeremiah 31:9), but the individual Jew apparently would never have thought to call God his personal Father. No wonder Jesus' claim to a special kind of sonship was considered blasphemous by his contemporaries.

Because God cares for each and every one of us individually, we should feel comfortable about ourselves and our lives; we should feel at home. Proclaiming God our Father is, in effect, our first implicit acknowledgment of peace as a consequence of faith. There is, of course, a sense of inner peace that comes from the profession of faith in the Son and in the Spirit, but inasmuch as our relationship to each of the divine persons is distinctive, the peace of each is unique and deserves mention in its proper place. Awareness of the Father's peace stems from our sense of belonging, of direction and purpose, of contentment in being.

The Provident Creator:
Shared Dominion under God

But the fullness of our sense of belonging is not reached in our acknowl-edgment of God's fatherhood alone; he is our Father almighty *and* the Creator of heaven and earth. In confessing faith in God as Creator as well as almighty Father, we express our confident belief in an all-powerful, benevolent, provident, and personal source of everything that exists. The phrase "heaven and earth," one of the images of completeness we use in our creeds, implies that creation is an ordered wholeness. There is nothing apart from God that did not have its beginning in him, is not sustained by him, and will not have its end in him.

The earliest stories of the Creator in our Jewish-Christian tradition are found, of course, in the opening chapters of the Bible. Two different mythic sources are represented in the accounts of creation in Genesis 1 and 2. Just as philosophers through the ages have argued to the existence of God from their awareness of order in the universe, so the priestly authors of the creation story in Genesis 1–2:4 use the sequence of days in the week to acknowledge both the majestic order in the mind of the Cre-ator and the miraculous harmony and wholeness of the created universe. God pronounces all of his creation *good*—sun and moon, sea and land, birds and beasts, man and woman. Everything has a place, and is arranged to be used and contemplated by humanity, created male and female in the image and likeness of God. On the sixth day of creation, God chooses freely, in an ineffable gesture of graciousness, to share dominion over the earth with humankind. Our dominion over creation under God has come to be referred to more simply as *stewardship*.

By contrast with the cosmic scope of Genesis 1, the narrative in Gen-esis 2:5–25, the older of the two stories, is down to earth, even earthy, pastoral in setting, and personal in tone. Man is formed by the Lord God from the dust of the ground and placed in a garden in Eden, one filled with beautiful trees, bearing fruit in abundance—but something is lacking. The Lord God recognizes that it is not good for the man to be alone, so he creates other living things—cattle, wild animals, and birds—in the hopes of finding a suitable companion for the man. Not until the Lord God takes a rib from the man's side and shapes it into a woman, however, does he find a true partner for him. The gift of a companion adds the contentment and happiness of human relationships to the gift of the garden itself, which implies both the need to work and considerable freedom, though this latter gift is limited. They must till the garden and care for it, and they can eat the fruit of any tree in the garden, except the tree of the knowledge of good and evil—an image that we will return to shortly when we discuss Genesis 3.

Whereas we associate a sense of security and wonder with our experience of God as provident Father, we understand the challenge of stewardship to be the consequence of our creaturely state as we obey God's command to "fill the earth and subdue it" (Genesis 1:28). With St. Paul, we labor daily to complete the creation that God has entrusted to us in Christ: "The whole created universe groans in all its parts as if in the pangs of childbirth" (Romans 8:22). But a steward's dominion is conditioned by the pleasure—the will—of his master, and also by the need to work responsibly with and for the others who share that dominion. Ours is clearly a limited dominion over the earth.

For conveying a realization of the limits of our dominion over the earth, Flannery O'Connor's short story "A Circle in the Fire" comes immediately to mind. A widow named Mrs. Cope, with an adolescent daughter, is comfortable enough by reason of the "rich pastures and hills heavy with timber" she owns, but like anyone with possessions, she worries, and her special fear is of fire in her woods. When three young delinquents from nearby Atlanta take a fancy to entertaining themselves in her woods and riding her horses, she shows just how poorly she copes with the burden of her farm. The youths confess that there is nothing as exhilarating to do in the concrete trap they live in, or any place as free and open and fresh as the property she owns. When they set fire to her woods out of sheer malice, and Mrs. Cope looks as if she has joined the dispossessed of the earth, it seems to be because she did not realize—as one of the boys instinctively knew—that "Gawd owns them woods and her too!" The statement, of course, has a double meaning, and so is doubly suited to enforce our understanding of stewardship. It means that God owns Mrs. Cope and her woods, *and* that she and God own the woods; and because the latter is true, her implied claim to absolute possession is doomed to disaster.

Pope John Paul II's encyclical letter *Laborem Exercens* ("The Priority of Labor") provides a detailed theology of human work and is appropriate reading in this context, especially Parts II and V, entitled respectively "Work and Man" and "Elements for a Spirituality of Work." It may well be the most distinctive of all of the papal encyclicals on the social order.

Building on the creation narrative in Genesis, and employing a personalist philosophy, the pope writes not just to address the worldwide oppression of laborers, but more fundamentally to define the call to stewardship as the indispensable ingredient of our nature as "persons": "Man has to subdue the earth and dominate it, because as the 'image of God' he is a person, that is to say, a subjective being capable of acting in a planned and rational way, capable of deciding about himself and with a tendency to self-realization."

In fact, as John Paul II insists, the human personality is essentially defined by work: "Only man is capable of work, and only man works, at the same time by work occupying his existence on earth. Thus work bears a particular mark of man and of humanity, the mark of a person operating within a community of persons." In other words, every person must work, whether with his hands or with his imagination, whether physically or intellectually, if he hopes to define himself as a person among persons.

Moreover, the value of the work that people do comes primarily from its significance for them and their self-realization (the subjective dimension) and not from what it is in itself (the objective dimension). "As a person he works; he performs various actions belonging to the work process. Independently of their objective content, these actions must all serve to realize his humanity, to fulfill the calling to be a person that is his by reason of his very humanity." And, amplifying his principle that "work is 'for man' and not man 'for work,'" the Holy Father adds: "Each sort [of work] is judged above all by the measure of the dignity of the subject of work, that is to say, the person, the individual who carries it out . . . even if the common scale of values rates it as the merest 'service,' as the most monotonous, even the most alienating work."

This encyclical on the importance, indeed necessity, of work in our lives as persons draws new meaning from two sayings of Jesus: "What does a man gain by winning the whole world at the cost of his true self?" (Mark 8:36) and "It is easier for a camel to go through the eye of a needle than for a rich man to enter the kingdom of God" (Matthew 19:24; Mark 10:25; Luke 18:25). It is not what we do or what we have that makes the difference, but *who we are*—which flows in large part from the significance of our work for us. Those who think otherwise have missed the essential challenge of stewardship. Moreover, all work is also with and for others as an expression of our communal obligation to family, society, and world to subdue the earth and thus complete the work of God's creation.

There is no greater literary advocate of the personal dignity of the worker than John Steinbeck, and perhaps no better fictional setting for the same concerns than his novel *The Grapes of Wrath*. Adapted for the screen by John Ford, it is perhaps the single most stirring presentation in American film of the quest for physical survival as well as of the solidarity of the workers of the world. We will have occasion to appeal to this novel in each of the subsequent sections of this book. Like all of Steinbeck's great novels, though, it laments the injustices done to workers and hence is an effective story of the Creator—one, too, in perfect sympathy with the fundamental insights of the papal social encyclicals.

In the middle of the Depression, and in the midst of a natural disaster—drought—the Joads leave their confiscated home and farm in Oklahoma's dust bowl and follow Route 66 west in quest of promised work picking grapes in California vineyards. Both novel and film follow their efforts to find the work that they need for the survival of their family, although the worldview of the novel is decidedly bleaker than the film's.

In the second-to-last shot of the film, a medium two-shot of Ma and Pa Joad through the windshield of their truck, emphasizing their bond as man and woman—possibly the most memorable scene of the film—Ma Joad says, "We'll go on forever, Pa, because we're the people." We realize then, if not before, that the most basic human bond lies in the universal fellowship of work, stemming from our shared dominion over the earth.

Stewardship Limited by Mortality

The peace and sense of purpose that come from knowing ourselves as creatures of a provident Father and Creator are tempered by the realization that our journey through life is limited, and not simply because of our measured dominion over the earth. The principal limitation on our lives in time is the unavoidable consequence of the kind of creature we are—namely, *bodied* spirits. Much of the data of human experience that has tormented the believing mind as evidence against the goodness of God—pain, disease, decay, death—and that constitutes the physical basis for the so-called "problem of evil" must candidly be placed in the context of creation. Pleasure and pain, ecstasy and death, are inseparable. If we want one, we must accept the other. One cannot sensibly blame God for the latter without praising him for the former. Better still, but this too anticipates later developments in the unfolding narrative of our creed, we can praise him for both and without the slightest fear of being guilty of fatalism, the sort of spiritual masochism that Catholics in particular are perennially accused of—unfairly.

Ironically, the peace that attends a realization of creaturehood is in part due to the very acknowledgment and acceptance of limitations. By contrast, the ancient Near East has left us in its earliest epic, *Gilgamesh*, tragic evidence of the dreary fate of a great man who refused to accept life's limits—even the partial insight that was available to him. Gilgamesh, who tamed the primeval forest and built the strong walls of Uruk, experienced his own mortality, as we all do, through the death of someone close to him: his dearest friend and companion in adventure, Enkidu. Instead of accepting the inevitable, Gilgamesh sets out on the impossible quest of immortality, one of the saddest journeys ever narrated because we know, as the original storytellers did, that it is doomed to frustration.

Gilgamesh seeks out Utnapishtim, a king of old who lives an endless life at the very edge of the known world, saved capriciously by one of the gods from a flood that destroyed the world and everything in it. If Utnapishtim's story has any moral for Gilgamesh, it is this: Who can account for the whims of the gods? For us, Utnapishtim's survival is the exception that proves the rule of morality. In one version of the story, Utnapishtim, against his better judgment, gives Gilgamesh a plant that will apparently assure his immortality (if he can preserve it), but the plant falls overboard in the passage back across the ocean and the snake that snatches it sheds its old skin for a new one (an ancient image of rejuvenation). Thus the quest for immortality eludes Gilgamesh as it does all of us.

Rollo May in *Love and Will*, writing from the depths of personal experience, both his and others' in crisis, says that we finally accept the limits of our own existence when we are individually touched by the trauma of disease. In his own case, he writes of understanding the value of the present moment and the urgent need to make each day count when the discovery that he had tuberculosis forced him to accept the fact that his days were numbered. Tommy Wilhelm in Saul Bellow's short novel *Seize the Day*, on the other hand, needs neither the death of a loved one nor the diagnosis of serious illness to come to grips with the squalor of his life. He is out of work, estranged from his wife, overly dependent upon his father, and duped by a con man out of his last savings. His life is a downward spiral till the moment he gets drawn into the movement of a line of mourners and finds himself dislocated, confused, peering down into the face of a dead stranger in an open coffin. Swept along by events, because of his own refusal to make even the simplest of choices for himself, he needs the vision in the mortuary chapel, his by chance, to know that life is not forever and that drifters are simply fools. What this novel helps us appreciate is the motivating force of limits perceived and accepted.

Other fiction comes to mind in this regard, like William Faulkner's *As I Lay Dying* and Flannery O'Connor's *The Violent Bear It Away*. But none perhaps is more precisely to the point or treats it as effectively and shockingly as O'Connor's short story "A Good Man Is Hard to Find." In it a perfect Southern lady, named simply "the grandmother," meets her match and more in the person of an escaped convict, who calls himself The Misfit—because nothing he ever did, he says, warrants the punishment he has suffered. A startling tale, but one that merits reading and rereading because of its profoundly Christian worldview, "A Good Man" shows us how The Misfit discovers the genuine goodness in the grandmother, buried under layers of gentility and cant, yet not until he has had her whole family killed—her son and daughter-in-law and two grandchildren—and is ready to kill her because she has made the mistake of recognizing him from the newspaper accounts of his escape from prison. Seeming to sense that her generation and social class were responsible, perhaps unwittingly but responsible nonetheless, for the injustices that made social outcasts out of people like The Misfit, she says finally, reaching out to touch her captor as he is about to shoot her, "Why, you're one of my babies. You're one of my own children!" Stunned more by her gesture than by her statement, The Misfit kills her, then concludes, "She would of been a good woman if it had been somebody there to shoot her every minute of her life." His statement can mean only one thing: it took the threat of death for the grandmother to show her true self.

Two fine films that deal with mothers' attempts to cope sensibly with the tragic, early deaths of their daughters are Herbert Ross's *Steel Magnolias* and James Brooks's *Terms of Endearment*; both films are instructive stories of the Creator because they remind us so poignantly of how short life seems and in some cases actually is, forcing us also to face the inevitable sense of missed opportunity that the death of a loved one confronts us with. What fiction of the sort we have just considered helps to nourish in us is a faith that accepts mortality as the source of our challenge to live fully here and now—to seize the day.

This discussion of death may seem to be premature in view of the sequence of the articles of the Apostles' Creed. The reason, though, for considering it in the context of creation is to make sure from the outset that we accept the kind of life we live—namely, one that is literally numbered in terms of years, days, hours, seconds. As it is often put ironically, death is a fact of life. When we acknowledge God as our Creator, we implicitly recognize ourselves as creatures of a certain sort, who live, breathe, eat, laugh, love, procreate, imagine, yearn—and die. The way in which we sensibly and peacefully, even amid tension, make each day of our lives count—and there are, of course, innumerable ways to do that, including not doing anything—will indicate how well we have also understood that other significant aspect of our creaturehood: our stewardship. The acceptance of limits and the challenge of stewardship go hand in hand. Only when we face the fact of death can we assume responsible dominion over creation.

Stewardship Hindered by Sin

Besides the limitations on our time, there is an even greater potential obstacle to our exercise of stewardship: the existence of sin in the world, not to mention its cumulative effect upon human history. The first part of the Apostles' Creed is silent about sin, even implicitly. In fact, the word appears only once, in the phrase "forgiveness of sin," in the midst of our confession of the Spirit. When it introduces our profession of faith in Jesus as "Christ" and "Lord," it simply assumes that we know the reason he was conceived of the Holy Spirit and born of the virgin Mary. The Nicene Creed, on the other hand, without mentioning sin explicitly, nonetheless proclaims early in our confession of belief in Jesus that it was "for us and for our salvation [that] he came down from heaven." Jesus comes to save us from our sins and from the sin of the world, to save us all from our worst selves—but this, too, is getting ahead of the narrative of our creed.

The Book of Genesis makes our divided selves in response to the challenge of creaturely dominion abundantly clear by introducing the story of the sin of our first parents within the context of the second account of creation. How are we, at this point, to understand "sin"? As stories go, there is of course none greater in all of our literature, both sacred and secular, than the story of the fall. The Lord God plants a garden in Eden and places in it the man that he had formed from the dust of the ground. Even before he provides him with animals and birds as partners, and then creates the woman from his rib as a more suitable companion, God gives the man an explicit command about the limits of his freedom to use the trees of the garden. "You may eat from every tree in the garden, but not from the tree of the knowledge of good and evil; for on the day that you eat from it, you will certainly die" (Genesis 2:16–17).

In disproportion to the brevity of this story, I have spent more time over the years trying to discover its meaning than of any other text that I have read or taught. No other mythic story has had a greater impact on the Western theological, literary, and artistic imagination, except perhaps the narrative of Jesus' passion and death. Its meaning, like all great literary texts, is obscured for us by the density and ambiguity of its symbolism. There is, of course, no general agreement about the nature of the sin of our first parents. The most obvious and universal, but least satisfying, explanation is to say that it was a sin of disobedience. It certainly is that, but if our understanding stops there, we all too easily make God's command seem like an arbitrary conflict of wills.

Why does the author of the sacred text provide us with so many other rich, though ambiguous details? Why is the man forbidden to eat of the fruit of "the tree of the knowledge of good and evil" and not of the "tree of life," that is also "in the middle of the garden"? Why introduce the element of the "crafty serpent" if sin is just a test of wills? Notice that the serpent knows there has been a limitation on the freedom of the couple, but either does not know what the limitation is or claims not to know. Why do the man and the woman realize that they are naked as soon as both have eaten the fruit of the forbidden tree? Note, too, that the Lord God, even though he asks the man if anyone had told him he was naked, immediately links their sensation of nakedness with eating from the forbidden tree. Why do the man and the woman fail to accept responsibility for their act? And why does God punish all three—the serpent, the woman, and the man? These are the key questions that need to be answered in some coherent way if an analysis of the story's meaning for us is to be complete.

To begin at the end and work backwards, it is clear that the structure of the inquisition and the sentencing following the Lord God's appearance in the garden *shows* us two things: both the innate tendency of humans to blame someone else for their mistakes, and God's insistence that all three are to blame for the offense. This venerable story, like all stories, normally *shows* us what we are to understand. I say *normally* shows because sometimes, as we shall see shortly, the author of a story does *tell* us his meaning, and when this happens we can see the distinction between the two methods of writing more clearly.

Once the man and the woman have eaten of the fruit of the forbidden tree, they instinctively feel shameful for their action. Being aware of their nakedness is a perfect image for the experience of shame, a public acknowledgment of the *social* nature of sin. Shame not guilt, which is interior, is the appropriate response to our awareness of our sinfulness. Prior to their sin, we had been *told* outright, "they had no feeling of shame towards one another," even though they were naked. They are also, understandably, fearful of the Lord God's approach in the cool of the evening.

The serpent provides the temptation. This image, as much as any other in the story, has caused problems over the centuries. The most consistent interpretation, both in art and in theology, has been to consider the serpent to be Satan, but the idea of Satan as a demonic figure was unknown in Israel at the time this narrative dates from. Recent biblical scholarship, moreover, appeals to the fertility cults of the Canaanites, and suggests that the Israelites, who preserved the story, would have seen the image of the serpent as a reference to the "brazen" idols of the infidels (e.g., 2 Kings 18:4). The serpent is called "more crafty than any other wild creature that the Lord God had made"; it is also one of creation's least attractive, indeed most frightening creatures. Later, in the punishment inflicted upon the serpent, it is clear that one of the purposes of the story was, as is so often the case with these primitive narratives, to explain the origin of some natural phenomenon—in this instance, why the snake crawls on its belly. (Recall the snake in *Gilgamesh* shedding its skin.) Let it suffice for our purposes to say that the image of the serpent is sufficiently associated with evil in the Hebrew imagination to be an appropriate image for a tempter. Moreover, in order to dramatize the temptation, it helps to have a character in the story, apart from the man and the woman, and for this reason, the serpent is personified and converses with the woman.

In fact, in its role as tempter, the serpent provides us with a clue that helps to unlock the symbolism of the story. He insists that not only will they not die when they eat of the fruit of the tree, they will actually "be like gods knowing good and evil." Because the tree is "the tree of the knowledge of good and evil," and they will be "like gods" if they eat its fruit, the imagery suggests that the *presumption* of claiming for themselves God's prerogative—to name good and evil—is at the heart of every sin. What else does our decision knowingly and deliberately to reject God's law say in effect? We know better than our Creator what is good for us. We would make ourselves the arbiters of morality rather than accept his revelation of what is and is not good for us as human beings. This interpretation of the story of the fall, therefore, considers the serpent an appropriate external reflector of the perversion of reason and will that sin entails.

Following hard upon the story of the fall is a record of sin's spread throughout the world. It would seem that the editors of the Book of Genesis wanted specifically, especially in the stories of Cain and Abel, Noah, and the Tower of Babel, to *show* how sin "begets" sin. This is, of course, the Bible's narrative version of the Christian doctrine of original sin, our name for the cumulative effect of the history of sin upon the world that we are born into and thus upon us even before we sin personally. Note that the account of the Tower of Babel—"with its top in the heavens" (Genesis 11:4)—again links sin with the presumption of wanting to be like gods; the heart of sinfulness lies in the denial of creaturehood, our radical dependence upon God.

How our own personal sins contribute to this continuing history of sin, making us all partners in the "sin of the world" (John 1:29), has been treated in a variety of classic cinematic and literary settings. In fact, novels and films that offer fictional variations on the impediment that original sin and its consequences pose for even our best efforts at stewardship seem to abound. Joseph Mankiewicz's film *All About Eve*, as the title itself suggests in using the Hebrew name for the mother of the race, is also, and more fundamentally, all about the fall. The temptress of this Eden is Eve Harrington, an aspiring actress who cons her way into the life and affections of the celebrated stage star Margo Channing with the idea, we come to discover, of supplanting her. Eve's companion in evil is the theater critic and cynic Addison De Witt, whose name alone is a reminder that this is no heavy-handed version of the fall from grace, but a clever, witty tale of demonic connivance—in the American literary tradition of humorous apocalypse, where the "last loosing of Satan" foreshadowing the end is portrayed in terms of the pervasive presence of the con artist. All are drawn unwittingly into Eve's scheme, except for Birdie, Margo's dresser, who remains skeptical of Eve throughout. In the middle of the film is the unmistakable signal of the director's intentions—a marquee announcing "The Devil's Disciple," just behind the theater where Margo's current hit is playing. When the film's final scene shows the process starting anew just as Eve, having achieved her goal, is conned by another young aspirant to the stage, we see the image of the new Eve multiplied tenfold in the mirrors she preens before. We are all the devil's disciples. In naming us "legion," the film clearly updates the biblical narrative of the history and universality of sin.

All the King's Men, Robert Penn Warren's Pulitzer Prize-winning novel about the rise and fall of an American demagogue, more than reminiscent of Louisiana's Huey Long, is also about the fall and its consequences, and as such it is surely a story of the creature, if not of the Creator. Warren's work is one of the masterpieces of modern American literature and deserves to be read, but the story is perhaps more accessible as adapted for the screen by Robert Rossen. Even though the film necessarily pales by comparison with Warren's complex novel, it is a powerful and justly honored work of art, winning three major Academy Awards—best picture, best actor (Broderick Crawford as Willie Stark), and best supporting actress (Mercedes McCambridge as Willie's mistress, Sadie).

In a tightly-crafted script, Rossen makes Willie the focus of dramatic attention, but filters his story through the viewpoint of Jack Burden, the novel's narrator. Aristocratic Jack Burden, a journalist sent to cover the political career of an opportunistic rural populist, is gradually drawn into the inner circles of power as events conspire to catapult Willie Stark into the State House. The thematic focus of the film as of the novel is on the "knowledge that kills": astute politician that he is, Willie is convinced that if you dig deeply enough, you can discover the dirt on anyone. "Man is conceived in sin and born in corruption," he insists; find the secret sin in a person's past and he becomes your pawn. When Willie orders Jack to discover "the dirt" on Judge Stanton, leader of the movement to have Willie impeached, the implied Humpty Dumpty of the title begins his fall from the wall of tyranny. About to be exposed, the judge takes his life; over his body stand Ann and Adam (his niece and nephew), Jack, and Willie. All gazes are on Willie at the heart of the frame, as at the center of a spider web—the novel's image for our human complicity in evil, and as fine an analogue for original sin as fiction has to offer.

In Elia Kazan's film *East of Eden*, Adam Trask, like our biblical first parent, has two sons: Cal (Cain) and Aaron (Abel). Similar again to the Genesis story, Aaron is favored by his father, while Cal is rejected. The film focuses on Cal's quest for a sense of personal dignity, which leads him to travel back and forth between the Monterey of his mother's bordello and the Salinas of his father's farm, between the shrouded coastline of white slavery and the sunlit valley of righteousness. The title, taken from Genesis 4:16, suggests that the dramatic action takes place "after the fall"; only the unfolding drama itself can tell us that it also occurs "because of the fall." Cal's rejection by his father is repeatedly emphasized, short of the final scene, by a visual composition of frames that shows him in angular contrast to—that is to say, at odds with—the physical world around him. Although the film foreshortens considerably the three-generation, east-to-west sweep of John Steinbeck's novel, it nonetheless consciously strives to make the Trask family a reflection of our biblical first family, whose story begins the Bible's account of the history of sin. When Adam finally accepts Cal as he is, impetuous, unruly, but devoted, the film confirms our belief that each of us, because of the effects of original sin, is a sad but hope-filled mixture of good and evil.

Structures of Sin:
Depleting Natural and Human Resources

One of the ways in which we continue to perpetrate the presumption of Eden, making ourselves "like gods," is by abusing and even destroying the resources of the earth; so before we conclude these reflections on stewardship, we should note, however obvious they may be, some of our greater actual sins against the earth and thus against one another, as well as some of the subtler ones—both of which we will find reflected in fiction. Sadly enough, in the course of human history, far too many people have thought that the portion of the earth they could grasp as their possession they could use as they would, as well as the human beings on it. Such were the tyrants and madmen of history. Today, though, rulers of an ever expanding number of countries control nuclear arsenals capable of destroying all the world or substantial portions of it, and too few of us consider them mad. We speak instead of national defense, and continue to risk the obliteration of mankind, while big business in the name of profits keeps workers in conditions of utter poverty and subjects peoples in developing countries to economic slavery.

Less obvious, but still frightening, because the majority of the people in industrialized societies seem to condone it—our greed for material things makes it necessary—there is today a vast silent partnership for the gradual destruction of the planet from the chemical and nuclear pollution of air, earth, and water. During the Gulf War, I remember seeing a bumper sticker that read "*Our* Chemical Industries are TERRIFIC," and I wondered what the rate of exchange was between the discovery of "better things for better living through chemistry," as one international firm used to boast, and the incidence of lakes and forests destroyed by acid rain, and rivers and streams polluted by toxic wastes. Perhaps "terrific" stood for "terrifying," but that may be too subtle a double entendre to expect from a bumper sticker.

When it comes to literature and film, there is, reasonably enough, little difference between the representation of the consequences of original sin (concupiscence or the inclination to sin) and original sin itself (universal patterns of sinfulness that affect each new generation coming into the world and that each new generation contributes to through its own sinfulness); both are presented as structures of sin in the image of Eden's original act of god-like presumption. In fiction as well as in reality, we violate stewardship by destroying human resources as well as natural resources. Two very recent war films have taken, on the whole, contrasting views of the destructive effects of World War II: Terrence Malick's *The Thin Red Line* and Steven Spielberg's *Saving Private Ryan*. Although I personally consider both films to be cinematic achievements of the highest order, I recommend each with a certain caution. Malick's film is considered by some critics to be too episodic and tediously long, and there is some merit to these complaints; Spielberg's, although praised for its consummate realism in depicting the invasion of Normandy, is suitable only for those who can tolerate the representation of extreme physical violence, designed however for the laudable purpose of helping contemporary audience's experience the utter insanity of modern warfare. Whereas Spielberg's film is edited for maximum visual and aural assault on the senses, Malick's most memorable images draw us into the serenity of the lost paradise of Guadalcanal before it became a battleground between American and Japanese forces.

Although there is a certain romanticism in its portrayal, the opening sequence of *The Thin Red Line* shows us a crocodile as it slowly submerges itself into a jungle pond, and shortly thereafter we see an American soldier, attracted to the island's primitive beauty, swimming in the same waters in Edenic harmony with all of nature. The image of a natural paradise is unmistakable; at the end, the soldier is dead as well as the crocodile. Between these framing sequences, the Americans invade the island and defeat its Japanese occupants; but before the battle is joined, there is another shot, more symbolic perhaps than realistic, of Marines climbing a hill to engage the enemy, before the first shot is fired, and watching in amazement as an island native walks past them going in the opposite direction. The meaning is clear: the natives and the unwanted occupants of the island, old and new, are working at cross-purposes. Not only are untold lives lost, the natural paradise is destroyed. It is the latter consequence of war that seems to dominate Malick's cinematic imagination.

Spielberg's *Saving Private Ryan* raises an ethical question that becomes the driving force of its narrative: How many men do you sacrifice to save one? After the Allies have pushed inland from the cataclysmic invasion of Normandy, eight men are sent on a mission to find Private Ryan, the only surviving brother of the four enlisted from an Iowa farm. Because the memory of the five Sullivan brothers killed in a single tragedy at sea is still very fresh in public memory, General George C. Marshall wants Private Ryan saved, apparently at any cost. The core of the film tells the harrowing story of his rescue, but once again it is the film's framing sequences that deliver its potent message.

The first thing we see is the American flag, spanning the wide screen, but its colors are muted. It seems old, faded, the remnant of a lost age—like the period of World War II when we felt pride rather than cynicism about its colors. In the last shot, the same Old Glory flaps in the breeze, then falls limp. Within these framing shots are parallel framing shots of an aging veteran, first falling on his knees before a grave in the military cemetery at Omaha Beach, sobbing, and at the end, begging his wife, "Tell me I was a good man." From the story of the rescue within the framing shots, we know this aging soldier to have been Private Ryan and the grave to be his rescuer's. Captain Miller's dying words to Private Ryan had been, "Earn this!" Have we lived this past half century, Spielberg asks, as if we deserved the sacrifice made for our freedom from Fascism, or have we squandered the peace earned at such a price? The tattered American flag more than suggests the latter.

Two other vastly different films in setting and tone, religious and artistic achievements of the highest order, deal predominantly with the senseless destruction of human resources: Roland Joffe's award-winning film *The Mission* and George Roy Hill's adaptation of Kurt Vonnegut's *Slaughterhouse-Five*. Near the end of Joffe's film, we have a direct confession of human involvement in the sin of the world, John's Gospel's term for original sin; the movie, however, is framed by images of collusion in destructive behavior. Although set in a Jesuit Reduction for the Guarani Indians in Paraguay in 1758, *The Mission* wants to be read, as its epigraph explicitly states, against the current climate of social and economic conflict in Latin America. In our context, it clearly demonstrates how our fathers' sins are visited upon us. The Reductions, often justifiably considered to be the most successful experiment in evangelization in the new world, were communities of mutual respect and love built on the pattern of the early Church, Jesuits and natives alike sharing the fruits of their physical and artistic labors. Complex patterns of sinful collusion in Europe, the old world, seal their fate. Spain and Portugal had recently signed a treaty that ceded Spanish territory, where several Jesuit reductions were located, to the Portuguese, who, still actively involved in the slave trade, did not want the Indians protected by the Reductions. Because the pope fears that he will lose Portugal's loyalty, he sends his emissary Cardinal Altamirano either to persuade the Jesuits to close the missions or to close them himself. The film begins and ends with his empty face filling the screen; only in the beginning does he speak, dictating his final report to the pope, with more than a touch of cynicism: "Your holiness, the little matter that brought me here to the furthest edge of your light on earth has now been settled, and the Indians are once more free to be enslaved by the Spanish and the Portuguese settlers."

In the film's penultimate sequence, we have the direct admission of collusion that I alluded to earlier. Cardinal Altamirano, reading the report of the destruction of the San Carlos mission, and most of its inhabitants, asks the Spanish and Portuguese envoys, "And you have the effrontery to tell me that this slaughter was necessary?" The Spaniard says nothing significant in his defense, except perhaps, "Yes." The Portuguese official adds, "We had no alternative, your Eminence. We must work in the world, and the world is thus." Altamirano's response is the sad confession of our continuing contribution to human history's sinful structures, "No, Señor Hontar, thus have we made the world," adding with precision and evident self-knowledge, "Thus have I made it."

Slaughterhouse-Five, Kurt Vonnegut's cult novel about a space-age Everyman who has come "unstuck in time," is a darkly humorous antiwar tale that mixes science fiction with historical fact. The totally unnecessary fire-bombing of Dresden in World War II—one of history's most tragic recent lapses into senseless destruction of human life and art—is the centerpiece of the novel's passionate plea for peace. As adapted to the screen by George Roy Hill, the presentation in sight and sound of the exquisite beauty of Baroque Dresden prior to the city's destruction is one of cinema's strongest antiwar statements. But in an encyclopedic way *Slaughterhouse-Five* manages to level its sights at the technological and personal excesses of an entire world, not unlike ours, that has substituted insanity for stewardship.

Billy Pilgrim, abducted by space travelers, spends his best moments on the planet Tralfamadore with the girl of his dreams, Montana Wildhack. The Tralfamadorans claim that humans are "bugs in amber," that any attempt to change reality is futile. The structure of the novel and film, however, runs counter to their philosophy. Inasmuch as Billy's ordeal as war prisoner from his capture behind the German lines to the fire-bombing of Dresden (that Vonnegut himself survived as a POW) is presented as a straight-line, although interrupted story, we are left with the clear impression that there are some atrocities against art and humanity that ought to be avoidable. The film's condemnation of human pretensions as well as its expression of hope are compellingly and tenderly conveyed in the warmth of the performances that George Roy Hill has drawn from his cast.

Responses to the Goodness of Creation: Wonder and Gratitude

To confess God as our almighty Father and Creator, as we have seen, means that we must have an enduring sense of belonging in a purposeful world and that we accept the limits and the challenge of our stewardship over it. In concluding these reflections on the first part of the Apostles' Creed, we must consider some fictional representations of the habitual dispositions that faith seeks to instill in us, such as profound gratitude and unending praise. Three recent American films fairly exude the sense of belonging and wonder that will nourish our gratitude for God's enduring goodness: Steven Spielberg's *Close Encounters of the Third Kind* and *Empire of the Sun,* and Philip Kaufman's *The Right Stuff.*

Close Encounters of the Third Kind is as richly textured and religiously satisfying a film as one could want. Three groups converge upon a mesa in Wyoming, with varying degrees of assurance that there will be an encounter with aliens: scientists, the United States government, and simple people capable of childlike wonder. Roy Neary, a utility worker in Muncie, Indiana, and a child named Barry from a nearby farmhouse are given special invitations. Government agents are present presumably because national security is threatened. The team of scientists has been collecting evidence of unexplained phenomena of disappearance and epiphany: World War II fighter planes in Mexico's Sonora Desert, a cargo ship in the Mongolian desert, and throngs of people in India pointing to the sky, chanting a five-note mantra. A pattern begins to emerge. The decoded musical notes point to a rendezvous with the extraterrestrial visitors at Devil's Tower, an allusion to the biblical high place where one encounters God. In his vision of the kindly and intelligent aliens, who communicate through music and gesture, Spielberg has achieved cinema's most profound representation of the ultimate benevolence of the universe. As the spaceship descends and its occupants emerge, the faces of those called to share the encounter show a mixture of fascination, wonder, and awe. The film's structure suggests the biblical pattern of election and response; its visual splendor instills that sense of childlike trust that comes through the revelation of benevolent purpose.

Spielberg's *Empire of the Sun*, based on J. G. Ballard's autobiographical novel, is about an adolescent boy's experiences as a Japanese prisoner during World War II. Separated from his parents and the security of his Shanghai cathedral school, Jamie Graham learns the art of survival from an American merchant seaman named Basie, who calls Jamie "Jim," giving him, as he says, "a new name for a new life." A thematic motif develops out of Jim's Latin lessons with the British physician who attends the camp's dying and who becomes the boy's genuine role model. (Among other things, he teaches Jim the art of resuscitation or, as Jim puts it, "how to bring people back to life.") In moments of distraction approaching delirium, Jim recites a jingle beginning with the perfect passive indicative of the verb *to love*, the tense in Latin that expresses the completion in present time of an experienced action. Jim's mantra—"*Amatus sum, amatus es, amatus est . . .*"—is intended no doubt as a revelation of his developing awareness of self. *He has been loved*—by his absent parents, by the physician, even by the degenerate Basie—and now, his apprenticeship completed and the war nearly over, it is time for him to love others. It is a curious apprenticeship in love, to be sure, yet one complemented by a bond of friendship that extends to the enemy, if the boy Kamikaze pilot who saves Jim's life—and whose death Jim cannot prevent—can be called an enemy in any sense.

Spielberg appeals once again to our sense of hierophany, but there are no encounters here with benevolent extraterrestrials, only the "everyday" epiphanies of an adolescent boy maturing in the midst of war, enthralled by the beauty of the Zero and the Mustang, and amazed by the courage of Kamikaze pilots. In the countryside, not too far from the camp of camouflaged Japanese soldiers awaiting the signal to take Shanghai, Jim sits in the cockpit of a downed Zero and marvels at the majestic flight of the model plane he has just launched (it seems preternaturally sustained in flight). The scene calls to mind Hopkins's ecstatic vision of "The Windhover"—"Brute beauty and valour and act, oh, air, pride, plume, here/ Buckle!" The film's final hierophany, accompanied by a magnificent choral "Laudamus Te," occurs as American planes drop lifesaving supplies to the dying prisoners. Spielberg shows us the world through a child's eyes of wonder. His images, to borrow one of Jim's favorite words, are "luxuriant."

Following Tom Wolfe's fascinating account of the early years of the American space program, Philip Kaufman's *The Right Stuff* takes a detached, almost ironic, often wryly humorous view of the proceedings. The gritty individualism of Chuck Yeager, the test pilot who broke the sound barrier but refused to be "Spam in a can," is juxtaposed with the schoolboy competitiveness of the college-educated flyers who were packaged by NASA as America's Mercury astronauts. Who has the right stuff, we are left wondering? Individuals like Yeager, without a doubt, the film claims, but the astronauts too, because they also possess that mixture of courage and determination that societies depend on in forging new frontiers. They are, our context suggests, stewards of our future, men building upon the challenge of nature. The omnipresent minister who brings sad tidings to the widows of dead test pilots and sings at their desert burials reminds us that there are definite limits to human endurance—and to our potential—but the film nonetheless extols the effort. Kaufman's visualization of the achievement of these pioneers in space leaves us with a clear sense of transcendent wonder, especially when sparks from an ancient aborigine's fire in Australia seem miraculously to engulf—and empower—John Glenn's endangered Mercury capsule, and when Gordon Cooper, surprised by the brilliance of the sun in space, exclaims in the film's last shot, "Oh Lord, what a heavenly light!"

Acknowledging God as Father and Creator, we should also be inclined always, in the image of the fictional Gordon Cooper, to praise his bounty and majesty reflected in the beauty of creation. Poetry is especially helpful for inspiring in us a sense of praise. No one has mastered the imagery of exaltation better than Gerard Manley Hopkins, Jesuit priest and poet of the late nineteenth century. Because he regularly fashioned new words to match his experience of faith, shifting from doubt to ecstasy, his poems are often difficult to understand. Two of his most accessible, though, are songs of praise, "God's Grandeur" and "Pied Beauty."

Although "God's Grandeur" laments our treatment of the earth—"all is seared with trade" (words that a century later ring in our ears like prophecy unheeded)—the poem celebrates the way creation keeps renewing itself.

The world is charged with the grandeur of God.
It will flame out, like shining from shook foil;
It gathers to a greatness, like the ooze of oil
Crushed. Why do men then now not reck his rod?
Generations have trod, have trod, have trod;
And all is seared with trade; bleared, smeared with toil;
And wears man's smudge and shares man's smell: the soil
Is bare now, nor can foot feel, being shod.

And for all this, nature is never spent;
There lives the dearest freshness deep down things;
And though the last lights off the black West went
Oh, morning, at the brown brink eastward, springs—
Because the Holy Ghost over the bent
World broods with warm breast and with ah! bright wings.

"The world is charged with the grandeur of God," Hopkins exclaims, taking his image of the *charge* from electricity, the use of which was becoming widespread at the time he was writing. God's majesty is also like the lightning shine of shaken goldfoil, he says, or like oil erupting from a crushed olive. To "reck his rod," which obviously we have not done, is to recognize the scepter of God's majesty. The images related to the effects of commerce all seem self-explanatory. Thus, even though generations of workers have worn the earth as bare as a footpath, "nature is never spent," the poet observes, because "there lives the dearest freshness deep down things." A prose writer would have said "deep down in things." And the freshness that Hopkins salutes is not only the evidence of God's greatness but also the result of the comforting presence of the Holy Spirit.

"Pied Beauty" begins, "Glory be to God for dappled things." Both *dappled* and *pied* refer to blotches of color. In succession, the poet praises God for skies streaked with clouds, rose-moles on trout, fire coals, finches' wings, and patches of landscape, then ends with a brief but beautiful declaration of faith and an exhortation:

Glory be to God for dappled things—
For skies of couple-colour as a brinded cow;
For rose-moles all in stipple upon trout that swim;
Fresh-firecoal chestnut falls; finches' wings;
Landscape plotted and pieced—fold, fallow, and plough;
And all trades, their gear and tackle and trim.

All things counter, original, spare, strange;
    Whatever is fickle, freckled (who knows how?)
      With swift, slow; sweet, sour; adazzle, dim;
He fathers-forth whose beauty is past change:
          Praise him.

The beauty of creation that Hopkins celebrates is dazzling in both color and design, a lavish reminder of the loving care and benevolent purpose God has bestowed on our earthly abode. There is not even a suggestion here of the ways in which our sins have obscured, even obliterated, the splendor of the natural world. Surely there is no better way to acknowledge our understanding of the significance of belief in God as both Father and Creator, and to inspire our determination to embrace one another in shared stewardship of the earth than by making our own the sentiments of this magnificent hymn of praise.

I believe in Jesus Christ, his only Son, our Lord.
He was conceived by the power of the Holy Spirit
and born of the Virgin Mary.
He suffered under Pontius Pilate, was crucified,
died, and was buried.
He descended to the dead.
On the third day he rose again.
He ascended into heaven,
and is seated at the right hand of the Father.
He will come again to judge the living and the dead.

God made the angels to show him splendor—as he made animals for innocence and plants for their simplicity. But Man he made to serve him wittily, in the tangle of his mind! If he suffers us to fall to such a case that there is no escaping, then we may stand to our tackle as best we can, and yes, . . . then we may clamor like champions . . . if we have the spittle for it. And no doubt it delights God to see splendor where He only looked for complexity. But it's God's part, not our own, to bring ourselves to that extremity! Our natural business lies in escaping. . . .

—Thomas More in Robert Bolt's *A Man for All Seasons*

II
Stories of the Savior

Daniel Coulombe, a young unemployed actor living in Montreal, is asked by a priest to update the passion play that is the principal attraction at a local Catholic shrine—quite obviously, although unnamed, the Oratory of St. Joseph sitting atop the mountain that gives the city its name. Four other aspiring actors, two women and two men, surviving in a variety of curious trades—working in a soup kitchen, dubbing foreign pornographic films, narrating a scientific documentary about the origins of the universe, and acting in television commercials that sell the body as well as the product—are drawn by Daniel into the research and collaboration that will yield their revised drama. How they complete the project and in the process Daniel becomes the *Jesus of Montreal* is, of course, the subject of Denys Arcand's excellent film of that name.

The group's rewritten passion story presents a Christ stripped of his divinity, the illegitimate son of a Roman soldier—reflecting some bizarre contemporary efforts to demythologize the Gospels. Nonetheless, the play as performed by the young actors retains enough of the intense drama of the biblical narrative to engage the audience that attends its opening night. Daniel's reputation as the Jesus of the passion play spreads quickly. However, Fr. Leclerc, who had commissioned the revision, is less than pleased with the merely human Jesus and, fearing the adverse reaction of his religious superiors, threatens to end their contract. Other more serious problems beset Daniel. While visiting Mireille, the actress who plays Magdalene, on the set of her television commercials, he objects to the way Mireille's body is being exploited for a beer ad. In a rage, Daniel destroys some television equipment in the studio—an appeal to Jesus' expulsion of the buyers and sellers from the temple. But here as elsewhere, it is Arcand's genius never to force the parallels in Daniel's life to the gospel story.

The second performance of the passion play ends with Daniel's arrest for destroying the studio's property; he refuses counsel and pleads guilty. Awaiting the decision of the judge in his case, and against Fr. Leclerc's orders, Daniel stages another performance of the passion play, which ends tragically. At the point of the crucifixion, police interrupt the play, telling the crowd to disperse and, in the melee that follows, Daniel is injured when the cross he is tied to is knocked to the ground. Taken to the hospital, Daniel seems to recover, but only long enough to wander through the subway with the two women from the troupe, preaching the catastrophic destruction of the city. Finally, he collapses and dies. Since he has no family, the women who are his friends and followers donate his heart and his eyes for transplants, which we are shown to be successful. The symbolism is perfectly clear. For Daniel, the organ transplants are a cinematic analogue of resurrection. Apart from his role in the passion play, Daniel, whose last name, Coulombe, means "dove," leads a life filled with analogies to the life of Jesus, many more obviously than I have alluded to here. He is, in fact, one of the most distinctive Christ figures in recent fiction.

Representations of Jesus and Stories of the Savior

Over the century, though, film has been particularly active in presenting us with representations of the story of Jesus that are much more faithful to the gospel narrative than Daniel Coulombe's passion play. Some of the very earliest feature films were actually episodic versions of the gospel story. There have also been many notable attempts to offer a realistic portrayal of the Gospels, with special emphasis usually on the passion narrative, all the way from Cecil B. De Mille's *The King of Kings* in 1927 to Franco Zeffirelli's *Jesus of Nazareth* in 1977. These works, however, invariably included some extra-biblical elements in an effort to appeal to their audiences or to tell a complete story. Even Pier Paolo Pasolini's masterful *The Gospel According to Saint Matthew* (1964)—the most faithful presentation of Jesus because it limited itself to a cinematic version of only one Gospel—included some material not found in Matthew's Gospel. Better than any of the others, Pasolini demonstrates the power of cinema to draw us into the narrative of Jesus' mission, as his moving camera tracks the intense, determined Jesus he portrays, always on the road toward Jerusalem, turning back to address his disciples—and us—lagging behind. Within this general category of "realistic" films about Jesus, we would have to place those marginal representations that are more fictional than evangelical. At the time of their release, they created a certain amount of controversy, precisely because of the liberties taken with their presentation of the gospel story. I am referring not only to movies like Martin Scorsese's *The Last Temptation of Christ*, based on the novel by Nikos Kazantzakis, but also to the two based on rock musicals, *Jesus Christ Superstar* and *Godspell*.

In the category of biblical epics such as *Quo Vadis?* and *The Robe*, with fleeting references to the gospel narrative, William Wyler's *Ben-Hur* stands alone, offering memorable images of rebirth and giving explicit testimony to the saving power of Jesus' passion and death. Wyler signals his theme of "the touch of life" by using Michelangelo's "Creation of Adam" as the background for the film's credits. Judah Ben-Hur, taken captive by the Romans and sent into slavery, is given water by a carpenter's son in Nazareth. Years later, he attempts to return the favor when Jesus is carrying his cross through the streets of Jerusalem, but his efforts are rebuffed by the Roman soldiers. In the stormy cataclysm that follows Jesus' crucifixion, Ben-Hur's mother and sister are cleansed of their leprosy. Michelangelo's "touch of life" becomes, with Jesus' death, a gesture of healing and new life.

Because our focus is on fiction's capacity to nourish faith, I will limit my discussion to those literary and cinematic works that, like Arcand's *Jesus of Montreal*, present us with purely fictional creations, yet characters who are given qualities unmistakably similar to those of the Jesus of the Gospels or whose stories have narrative developments reminiscent of the scriptural story. These characters in fiction are the ones who have traditionally been called Christ figures. I have chosen, for reasons of symmetry with the other parts of this book, to refer to them as savior figures and to their fictional settings as stories of the Savior. Stories of the Savior, generally speaking, provide fictional responses to Huston Smith's second fundamental religious question—Is salvation a matter of the head or of the heart?—that are consonant with the faith of the Apostles' Creed, which implicitly looks to the heart as the locus of sacrificial love.

Passion:
Redemptive Value of Unavoidable Suffering

The extent, however, to which suffering and especially death are to be entertained as consequences of faith's commitment in love has traditionally been assigned carefully defined limits by both theologians and imaginative writers. The following passage from Teilhard de Chardin's *The Divine Milieu* provides a perfect complement to Robert Bolt's fictional presentation of Thomas More's determination to try to escape conviction by the courts of England, that is the epigraph to this chapter.

It is a perfectly correct view of things—strictly consonant with the Gospel—to regard Providence as concerned throughout the ages with the prevention and tending of the wounds of the world. It is in truth God who raises up the great doctors and the great benefactors of the human race in the course of time and in conformity with the general rhythm of progress. It is He who prompts even the most unbelieving to search after all that comforts and all that cures. And surely men recognize the divine Presence instinctively, in the fact that hatreds are appeased and disagreements unravelled in the presence of those who free the body and the mind. Can there be any doubt of it? At the first approach of the diminishments, we cannot hope to find God except by loathing what is coming upon us and doing our best to avoid it. The more we repel suffering at that moment, with our whole heart and our whole strength, the more closely we cleave to the heart and action of God.

This is, of course, exactly what Thomas More tells his family that he intends to do when confronted by the text of Henry VIII's Act of Succession. As a lawyer, but more fundamentally as a human being who knows that he is called to serve God "wittily, in the tangle of his mind," he looks to see if some wording in the law might permit him to take the oath of allegiance to his king and yet not deny his higher commitment to the pope, and so avoid certain death on the gallows. For Teilhard de Chardin, the term *diminishment* seems to cover any setback in the evolutionary process, most notably trials, tribulations, pain, and suffering of any sort. Even though we act in God's image when we avoid suffering or eradicate its causes, the true test of faith occurs when even our noblest efforts cannot prevent it. Then we discover that it is God's will that we suffer, even as Jesus, after praying in the garden that the cup of suffering pass him by, surrendered himself willingly to his captors. This is the moment in which Teilhard de Chardin—and by implication Thomas More—believes that we truly encounter and, hopefully, embrace the passion and death of Christ.

Cool Hand Luke, *The Outlaw Josey Wales*, and *The Last Picture Show* are three perennially popular films, all better known than the novels they are adapted from, that make clear statements about the redemptive value of unavoidable suffering; as stories of the Savior, although, they are more reminiscent of Isaiah's suffering servant who bears the burdens of the nation than of the Jesus of the Gospels who conquers death. In each case the victim of suffering is a fictional character whose status in society—a convict, an outlaw, and a pool-hall operator—would seem initially to argue against his consideration as a savior figure.

In Stuart Rosenberg's *Cool Hand Luke* (based on the novel by Donn Pearce), Lucas Jackson or Luke, as he prefers to call himself, is played so convincingly by Paul Newman that one wonders whether the character's status as a savior figure is not mainly a factor of Newman's performance. Luke, an obvious nonconformist, was "mostly just settling an old score," he explains later, when he is caught cutting the heads off parking meters. His crime is perhaps no worse than a drunken act of civil disobedience. Luke's presentation as a savior figure is as indirect as any major Hollywood film variation on this theme. There are, however, a couple of obvious but unexpectedly placed images of crucifixion. After Luke, on a dare, eats fifty hard-boiled eggs, he lies exhausted on a tabletop with arms outstretched, his body a classic image of the pose of the crucified. In the film's final shot, the camera withdraws from the place where Luke's "disciples" are working, providing a helicopter view of a crossroads as inverted cross.

Luke's resistance to the inhumanity of the chain gang is a subtle reminder of how Jesus challenged the oppressive social structures of his day. Luke tells his mates early on that all he hears at the correctional station is "a lotta guys laying down lots of rules and regulations." The cruelest of all the captain's decisions is to put Luke in "the box"—the chain gang's outhouse-style place of solitary confinement—when word arrives that Luke's mother has died; it is a warning for him not to think of escaping. The boss who puts Luke in confinement apologizes in language reminiscent of Adolf Eichmann, "Just doing my job, Luke," to which Luke responds, "Call it your job doesn't make it right, boss." After Luke has escaped twice and been caught twice, he is made repeatedly to dig and then fill his own grave. His body exhausted, but his spirit never broken, Luke responds, "Ain't no grave gonna hold my body down!"—the film's only hint of resurrection.

Luke's last agony, in an ironic variation on the passion narrative, is not in a garden, but in an abandoned church. Luke's "Why have you forsaken me?" is a dialogue with God, silent in his house, that begins with, "Anybody here?" Dragline, Luke's companion on his third and final attempt to escape, is a confused Judas who turns Luke over to the pursuing bosses, thinking that they will spare his master. Sensing the betrayal, Luke stands in the church door and defiantly, but with his typical smile, addresses the positioned bosses, returning the captain's—and the film's—most famous line, "What we got here is [a] failure to communicate!" He is shot instantly and dies on the way to the prison hospital, we are led to believe, because the captain knows that he cannot survive the hour's ride.

The final scene shows the other prisoners fondly recalling Luke's rebellious smile and apparently determined to resist oppression themselves as a result of Luke's example, his willingly accepted suffering and death.

If a convict seems an unlikely savior image, a western "outlaw" may seem even less so. However, Clint Eastwood's *The Outlaw Josey Wales*, based loosely on Forrest Carter's novel *Gone to Texas*, presents a man who like Job (and of course Jesus) suffers unjustly and who, in the pattern of the western "outlaw" who is really an instrument of justice in a lawless land, avenges the injustice. Renegade soldiers, known as "red legs," raping and pillaging the settlers on the plains in the final days of the Civil War, take Josey Wales' wife captive and burn down the house his young son is in. After burying the charred body of his son, Josey places a makeshift cross over the grave, praying in the words of Job, "Ashes to ashes, dust to dust; the Lord giveth and the Lord taketh away." In agony, he collapses under the cross, seeming to take its burden on his shoulders, with one arm of the cross stuck in the ground reminiscent of Jesus' fall under the weight of the cross on the way to Golgatha. Although he sets out to take justice in his own hands, the film suggests that it is not until Josey experiences the corruption of the senator and the army officer in control of the territory that he feels fully justified in his own mission. The strongest indication of his messianic role is shown, though, not in his fighting for justice, but rather in his ability to attract "the lowly" of the earth to his side and to lead them, as it were, into the promised land—an innocent youth, a Cherokee chief, a brutalized squaw, and a Missouri family en route to claim its inheritance in Texas.

The Last Picture Show, a novel by Larry McMurtry that was adapted for the screen by Peter Bogdanovich, is a story of the savior that relates the necessity of suffering to the acquisition of wisdom. The film is a minor masterpiece and deserves viewing for the performances alone, especially Ben Johnson's Academy Award portrayal of Sam the Lion, the story's suffering servant. The setting is the small Texas town of Anarene that, in the early 1950s, like so many rural stops on the way west, is losing both its population and its traditional social and moral core. Although there is a considerable amount of explicit sexual material in the film, it is in no way erotic, and much of it is actually rather humorous. In fact, in the film's severe black-and-white contrasts, it will actually seem quite tame alongside the needlessly explicit and often excessive contemporary representations of sex. Bogdanovich, following McMurtry, uses the pattern of sexual liaisons strictly as a metaphor for the frantic, bumbling attempts of the young to reach out for solid moorings in the chaos of disintegrating social structures.

Sam the Lion owns Anarene's three public places—the cafe, the pool hall, and the movie theater—where the youth of the town of necessity gather. By the time we meet him, though, Sam is more a lamb than a lion, a meek, long-suffering man who takes a paternal interest in the town's youth, but is capable of stern discipline when the occasion warrants it. Although we never learn the precise nature of his suffering, he is clearly Anarene's sole source of values. Only with Sam's untimely death do we discover the nature of his wisdom.

Lois Farrow, the mother of the town tease and herself apparently a recovering tease, tells Sonny, Sam's ward, about her indebtedness to Sam. "If it hadn't been for him," Lois admits, "I would have missed it, whatever it is." Despite Lois's inability or refusal to name "it," the film's context makes it perfectly clear that "it" is the experience of genuine love and, by implication, of God. The wisdom that Sam learned through suffering was the need to respect and engage others as persons rather than use them as objects for one's transient satisfaction. Lois's encounter with the divine is fortunately more enduring than Blanche DuBois's in *A Streetcar Named Desire*. Sam's selfless love has saved Lois from despair, and the memory of his example, we presume, will have a lasting effect on Sonny as well. It is the challenge of wisdom gained through honest suffering, the film suggests, that is our last, best hope for survival in a world of rapid social change. It may well be our last, best hope at any time, in any place.

Variations on the theme of redemptive sacrifice can be found in two classic westerns that are considered masterpieces of the genre—Fred Zinnemann's *High Noon* and George Stevens's *Shane*, movies that are associated more in the popular memory with their lead actors, Gary Cooper and Alan Ladd respectively, than with their directors. Both films exemplify the uniqueness of the savior figure in fiction. What makes Will Kane in *High Noon* and Shane savior figures is not the perfect symmetry of their stories with the gospel narrative, but rather the fact that each possesses personal qualities associated with Jesus or acts in a manner that reflects the pattern of his ministry. Will Kane interrupts his wedding day to defend the town he had been sheriff of—and himself—from a vicious killer, just released from prison, who will return at "high noon" to take his vengeance. Like Jesus abandoned by his own apostles, Kane ultimately faces his nemesis alone. Shane, on the other hand, typical of the mysterious rider-marksman who appears out of nowhere, acts as the catalyst who quietly unites some settlers in their efforts to fight off the local, ruthless cattle baron. His work accomplished, he rides away over the hills, never to be seen again.

Self-sacrifice is a theme in movies that happily, for the believer, transcends genres. Who can watch *Casablanca*, for instance, without being moved to want to sacrifice self for a noble cause? If love of a woman can draw the cynical Rick Blaine out of self-serving isolation, surely Jesus' infinite compassion can transform the most hardened heart. Although there are some aspects of Michael Curtiz's film that seem overly sentimental by more recent (although regrettably rare) standards of film excellence, the brilliance of the performances, especially by Humphrey Bogart and Ingrid Bergman, has easily survived the passage of time since World War II. Sidney Lumet's *Serpico* demonstrates the capacity of one man to confront the evils of an institution. A street-wise undercover New York policemen, acting out of disgust for injustice rather than love, nonetheless demonstrates the courage that leads an individual to risk everything for what he believes in.

Death:
Self-Sacrifice in Remembrance of Him

One of the most challenging insights into the redemptive value of suffering that I have ever encountered in my reading is in Quentin Quesnell's *This Good News*, a splendid exercise in biblical theology. Quesnell says that we experience the paschal mystery of our redemption precisely when our most conscientious, grace-driven efforts to serve others in the pattern of Christ—that is, to serve the downtrodden, the lowly, the outcasts of society—meet with scorn, rebuffs, persecution and even, although rarely, death. When we discover that, despite our best efforts to the contrary, our lives have become a sign of contradiction, we are most like Christ through the grace of his Spirit. It was the quality of Jesus' love, Quesnell points out, that led to his crucifixion and death. This understanding of the paschal mystery amplifies Teilhard de Chardin's concept of "diminishments" and the function in our lives of the suffering that we cannot escape; it is also in the spirit of Robert Bolt's portrayal of Thomas More's martyrdom, for he makes love the ultimate motivation behind More's allegiance to the pope over his king and thus, as we have seen, the only reason his death will make sense.

Why should love, of all things, provoke conflict and lead to suffering and death? No doubt if we were able to answer this question with any kind of precision, we would have probed the heart of the paschal mystery itself. Our context permits perhaps only the hint of an explanation, based on the apparent dynamics of the gospel narrative. By serving the needy, the downtrodden, the lowly, the outcasts of society—in fidelity to the spirit of God's kingdom whose coming he preached—Jesus clearly challenged the social structures of his day. "Come to me, all whose work is hard, whose load is heavy; and I will give you relief" (Matthew 11:28). In mixing freely with lepers, prostitutes, tax-collectors, unbelievers, even hated Samaritans, Jesus angered the scribes and the Pharisees, and their anger developed into open conflict. His efforts to show that laws were made for people and not people for laws—even the Law—effectively challenged the very heart of contemporary Judaism. As his following grew, and the confrontation with the Jewish leaders intensified, the Romans became concerned about the preservation of order in the territory. The rest of the tragic story is recorded clearly in the concluding narratives of the Gospels: Pontius Pilate succumbed to the persuasion of the Jewish priests and elders, and had Jesus crucified. There were, therefore, social, religious, *and* political reasons why Jesus' efforts to establish the Kingdom of God—his preaching and his actions—led inevitably to the cross.

How does Jesus' death bring about our redemption? Simply to ask the question seems presumptuous in the extreme because we are obviously dealing with a profound mystery. Many explanations have been advanced by the Fathers and great theologians of the Church. Every age, though, must seek its own and, indeed, it is the assumption of this book that each of us must probe the mystery and seek to understand the way it affects and effects our own lives.

There is, it seems to me, no more practical demand of our faith than this, or more obvious place to seek an understanding of it than in our celebration of the Eucharist. We gather together as a community of believers because Jesus, in sharing bread and wine at his last Passover meal with his apostles, instructed them: "Do this in remembrance of me." At the heart of our eucharistic celebration, therefore, is our memorial of his sacrificial death and our ritual reenactment of it. Jesus, master and teacher, indeed always the masterful teacher, asks us to break bread together and share the cup of blessing. He has, moreover, dictated the special meaning—the new reality—of this ritual action. The breaking of the bread is the visible, memorial presence of his broken body; the pouring of the cup of wine, our acceptance of his blood shed for the remission of our sins.

Does it not make sense to say that Jesus, in placing this memorial of his death at the heart of our union and communion as an assembly of faith, urges us, as often as we participate, to realize that unless our wills are broken and our lives' energies poured out, we are not loving our neighbor in need—and him therefore—as he has made it possible for us to, through the radical grace of our redemption?

This is surely what St. Paul has in mind when he admonishes the Corinthians about their reported behavior at their memorial celebrations (1 Corinthians 11:17–32). Because they refuse to "wait for one another," fall into "sharply divided groups," and fail to share their food and drink with their "poorer members," they are being "contemptuous of the church of God" and, quite pointedly he adds, they are "desecrating the body and blood of the Lord." "A man must test himself," St. Paul urges, "before eating his share of the bread and drinking from the cup. For he who eats and drinks, eats and drinks judgment on himself if he does not discern the Body." We do not "discern the Body" if we fail to see the Lord himself in the presence of his followers, the Church. Conversion, a fundamental change of heart, is the "test" necessary for proper participation in the Eucharist.

Saint Matthew's account of the Sermon on the Mount also has a pointed warning about the changed disposition we should have toward one another in approaching the altar, and even though it would be anachronistic to think that Jesus' instruction is directly referring to the Christian communion table, there is no doubt that the saying has profound implications for our participation in the Eucharist; it most probably reflects the eucharistic catechesis of the early church. "If, when you are bringing your gift to the altar, you suddenly remember that your brother has a grievance against you, leave your gift where it is before the altar. First go and make your peace with your brother, and only then come back and offer your gift" (Matthew 5:23–24).

Within our communities of faith, we are bound together, by the grace of this memorial, in the image of selfless love. Thus, if our love is not making a difference in the world, we have not awakened to the fullness of the eucharistic challenge. If our love is not provoking a response—indeed, if it has not become a "scandal" as Jesus' liberation of the oppressed became—then we have not as yet allowed the grace of his redemptive death to work its miracle in our hearts. And who of us can say that this is not the case? It is our normal inclination to shrink from the challenge of self-sacrifice. Is it the inevitable final conflict that we are too cowardly to embrace? Perhaps!

If we recall, though, the first question that we asked—Why should love provoke conflict and lead to death?—it is clear that our discussion thus far has tended to confirm *the fact* that this was the case with Jesus' redemptive love by showing *how* conflict and death resulted from his love. *Why* this is the pattern of our redemption remains hidden in the mystery of God's loving plan for our salvation. The paradox of Christianity is none-theless implicit in our discussion: the conflict that resulted from Jesus' love and that led to his death brought about a higher level of human unity and community. These are the facts recorded in the Acts of the Apostles: as a result of Jesus' death and resurrection, we witness the miraculous spread of belief in Jesus Christ through the preaching of the apostles and their efforts to form new communities of faith and love.

Within the last century, there have been two great popular movements inspired by Jesus' life, based on a philosophy of nonviolent protest: Gandhi's quest for India's independence from British rule, and Martin Luther King's Civil Rights Movement in the United States. In both instances, again in the pattern of Jesus' redemptive death, conflicts resulting from the nonviolent protests led to the assassination of the leaders of the movements. Yet who can doubt that both countries—despite continuing injustices—are infinitely better off today, socially and politically, than they were before their lead-ers' deaths? Obviously, as we reflect upon our lives and discern honestly the weakness, even absence, of our generosity, we must beg for the grace to be open to the challenge of the eucharistic memorial, to know when, where, and how in our daily lives we must expend our time and energy— our selves—for the sake of others, especially those who have most need of our love.

We are not, however, all Gandhis or Kings, to say the least; indeed, we do well to believe that theirs was a special prophetic, almost messianic, gift. For most of us, the normal way of self-sacrifice will be, at best, a pale reflection of the Little Way of St. Thérèsa of Lisieux, the Carmelite nun who, although anxious to be a missionary and to do great things for God in foreign lands, was forced by illness to remain in the convent. She never-theless achieved great sanctity in a short time by seeking God's will in the most menial everyday tasks. Novelist and essayist Walker Percy, who died in 1990, left a marvelous fictional tribute to the Little Flower, as St. Thérèsa has come to be called, in his first novel, *The Moviegoer*. Binx Bolling, the moviegoer of the title, far from seeking a model of perfection, is sunk in the malaise of everyday existence and actually not far from despair. "The search," he believes, provides a way out of the malaise, but ways into the search are unpredictable. When he finally admits that "it is not a bad thing to settle for the Little Way" and speaks about the possibilities for action open to him, he is not referring explicitly to St. Thérèsa, but it sounds remarkably like her Little Way. "There is only one thing I can do," he tells his fiancée, "listen to people, see how they stick themselves into the world, hand them along a ways in their dark journey and be handed along, and for good and selfish reasons. It only remains to decide whether this vocation is best pursued in a service station or . . ." He is interrupted by Kate's suggesting the other alternative, "Going to medical school?" Binx's phrase "for good and selfish reasons" is his modest, and appropriate, way of denying any claims to sanctity. In the context of the eucharistic memorial, we would all be far better off if, through the grace of the sacrament, we gave ourselves unselfishly in simple, everyday ways to those in need *within our reach*.

Literary reflections of the centrality of the Eucharist in our lives of faith—and of the redemptive effect upon us of our ritual memorial of Jesus' sacrifice—are rare and necessarily indirect because that is the way of fiction, but they do exist and we can profit greatly from them. A wonderfully touching film that far too few people have seen, Glenn Jordan's *Mass Appeal* based on a play of the same name by Bill Davis, pairs an idealistic but confused young seminarian with a priest who is all too complacent in his role as pastor of a devoted flock. Mark Dolson is assigned as an apprentice to Fr. Farley by the rector of the seminary precisely because Farley is a respected preacher. His Mass, as the title puns, appeals to the masses: Farley "dialogues" with his congregation, but his traditional theology makes no demands. He is easy on himself, easier still on his flock. On the level of the film's witty dialogue, the apprenticeship pits a "Bangladesh granola-head" seminarian against a "song-and-dance" theologian. When Dolson, with the honesty typical of his generation, admits his sexual ambivalence—although firm commitment to celibacy—while defending two seminarians accused of a homosexual involvement, the rector takes action to dismiss Dolson too from the seminary. Convinced of Dolson's sincerity, Farley delivers an impassioned plea to his parishioners to join him in fighting the rector's decision. As a result of their conflict over the effect that preaching the Word should have on others, it is clear that the two men have had a profound effect on one another. Farley drinks less and cares enough to get politically involved, and Dolson discovers that he may be able to challenge the masses without saying Mass. Although the focus of the conflict is on preaching, the liturgical setting implicitly appeals to the saving action of the Eucharist—and to the Little Way of helping those within our reach.

There is, I think, no more profound presentation of the centrality of the Eucharist to our life of faith than in Flannery O'Connor's novel *The Violent Bear It Away*. In a letter to one of her friends, she describes a dinner party she had attended at which the conversation turned to the Eucharist and her hostess called the communion wafer "a symbol," as if to say that it was *just* a symbol. O'Connor writes that she responded "in a very shaky voice, 'Well, if it's a symbol, to hell with it'" She goes on to explain to her friend: "That was all the defense I was capable of but I realize now that this is all I will ever be able to say about it, outside of a story, except that it is the center of existence for me; all the rest of life is expendable." In addition to her marvelous profession of faith, she has also provided us with the novel *The Violent Bear It Away*.

Since O'Connor was attracted to the directness, even fanaticism, of fundamentalist prophets, it is not of course the sacramental ritual itself that her novel set in rural Georgia deals with, but rather the image for the Eucharist in John's Gospel, "the bread of life." The main character, a fiery backwoods preacher named Mason Tarwater, who ironically has died before the novel begins, is convinced that he has sown the seed of God's Word in his grandnephew, referred to simply by his last name, Tarwater. It is clear that Mason intends the boy to carry on his ministry to the Word. The seed that Tarwater resists with all his determination, but ultimately allows to sprout in his soul as a free acceptance of the prophetic call, had from his earliest consciousness of it, we are told, aroused in him a hunger for "the bread of life."

O'Connor's masterful use of the Johannine imagery makes perfect sense not only in the fundamentalist setting of her fiction but also in the hearts of her readers who share an attraction to the eucharistic meal. "The boy sensed that this was the heart of his great-uncle's madness, this hunger," the narrator explains, "and what he was secretly afraid of was that it might be passed down, might be hidden in the blood and might strike some day in him and then he would be torn by hunger like the old man, the bottom split out of his stomach so that nothing would heal or fill it but the bread of life." Whenever Mason would remind him that "the servants of the Lord Jesus could expect the worse" but their reward in the end would be the bread of life, "the boy would have a hideous vision of himself sitting forever with his great-uncle on a green bank, full and sick, staring at a broken fish and a multiplied loaf."

At the end of the novel, Tarwater seems to see and accept the very vision that Mason had instructed him to seek, as he looks across the field near the burned-out ruins of their house. The eucharistic imagery becomes, at this point, an anticipation of the heavenly banquet:

> [The field] seemed to him no longer empty but peopled with a multitude. Everywhere, he saw dim figures seated on the slope and as he gazed he saw that from a single basket the throng was being fed. His eyes searched the crowd for a long time as if he could not find the one he was looking for. Then he saw him. The old man [Mason] was lowering himself to the ground. When he was down and his bulk had settled, he leaned forward, his face turned toward the basket, impatiently following its progress toward him. The boy too leaned forward, aware at last of the object of his hunger, aware that it was the same as the old man's and that nothing on earth would fill him. His hunger was so great that he could have eaten all the loaves and fishes after they were multiplied.

Even though *The Violent Bear It Away* is backwoods fundamentalist in the details of its setting, it is one of the most profoundly Catholic novels ever written. In acknowledging our hunger for the bread of life, we implicitly profess our faith in the redemptive effect of the Eucharist as the memorial of Jesus' total gift of self.

Walker Percy, on the other hand, uses traditional Catholic settings in all of his novels, but his imagery is more elusive than O'Connor's. An engaging aspect of his fiction from a religious perspective is the way he associates major insights or experiences of conversion, not just with the liturgical calendar (e.g., with important Christian feast days, as many great writers have done), but with the eucharistic liturgy itself. This is particularly true in his two novels about Dr. Thomas More—*Love in the Ruins* and *The Thanatos Syndrome*. Percy's self-confessed "bad Catholic" is intentionally named after the saint, who in the fictional portrait of Robert Bolt has become for us a norm of faith's perfect commitment.

The representation of the process of reconciliation in *Love in the Ruins*—which is also the novel's climactic moment of truth—comes just before Midnight Mass on a Christmas Eve five years into the new age that follows the story's averted apocalypse. (The lengthy subtitle of the novel is *The Adventures of a Bad Catholic at a Time Near the End of the World*.) Dr. Thomas More, by a most tortuous path, comes finally to admit that he experiences sorrow, or at least shame, for his sins, but it is only after a prolonged examination of his attitudes by his confessor. After accusing himself of "drunkenness, lusts, envies, fornication, delight in the misfortunes of others, and loving [himself] better than God and other men," More tells Fr. Smith that he feels no sorrow, then acknowledges that he feels sorry for "not being sorry," and later says that he will pray for sorrow. His exasperated confessor, after laboring hard to elicit contrition from him and appearing ready to bring the session to an end, says at last (as More narrates it):

> "Meanwhile, forgive me but there are other things we must think about: like doing our jobs, you being a better doctor, I being a better priest, showing a bit of ordinary kindness to people, particularly our own families—unkindness to those close to us is such a pitiful thing—doing what we can for our poor unhappy country— things which, please forgive me, sometimes seem more important than dwelling on a few middle-aged daydreams."
> "You're right. I'm sorry," I say instantly, scalded.
> "You're sorry for your sins?"
> "Yes. Ashamed rather."
> "That will do."

That More is *scalded* finally by images of possibilities, of the good things he has failed to do, rather than by an analysis of his misdeeds, is not surprising. He is, after all, preparing to participate in the Christmas liturgy, the remembrance of the new creation that would, through Jesus' death on the cross, reveal the boundless possibilities of selfless love. Nor is it surprising that Fr. Smith's suggestions for More's new beginning resemble the Little Way that Walker Percy seemed so devoted to; new beginnings are often quite modest.

At the end of *The Thanatos Syndrome*, a sequel to *Love in the Ruins*, the Eucharist is once again the occasion for hope, the signal for a call to service, however modest. Like *Love in the Ruins*, this novel too has a not-so-distant futuristic setting: a time in American life when the Supreme Court, in its ruling on *Doe v. Dade* (a barely disguised reference to *Roe v. Wade*), "permits the 'termination by pedeuthanasia' of unwanted or afflicted infants, infants facing a life without quality"—Percy's satirical projection of an American world ironically similar to the Weimar Republic and the Third Reich, when German and Austrian doctors "disposed" of people with hopeless diseases or birth defects that rendered them useless to society (all this too before the Holocaust). Tom More, still a Catholic, but not nearly as bad as he claimed to be in the earlier novel, having discovered odd patterns of behavior among his psychiatric patients and eventually exposing a secret criminal experiment in human behavior by health care "professionals" in his area, faces a choice about his future (either to work at a nearby psychiatric facility or to take the directorship of a hospice), when his wife, Ellen, comes to his office to tell him that he has received a phone call from Fr. Smith, now a patient at his own hospice. More assists the priest at Mass occasionally when his regular server, Milton, is too ill to do so. Ellen, however, thinks that it is an invitation to meet the new king and queen of Spain, who are visiting New Orleans. More recounts the conversation with his wife in this fashion:

> "The priest wants you to meet them out there. Tomorrow."
> "I see" . . .
> "He only gave me three hints. Royalty, a visit, gifts and—a Jewish connection" . . .
> "That's four."
> "Right. Now get this. I happen to know that the new queen [of Spain], Margarita, has Jewish blood. . . . "
> "I see."
> "Tomorrow morning at eight—why eight I don't know." She's briskly writing down the appointment. "Out there."
> "Very good," I say as briskly, frowning to keep from smiling.
> "Why don't you call him and tell him I'll be there."
> "Don't you worry." She's already on the phone.
> What Father Smith has told her and she me without knowing it is that he needs me tomorrow morning. Milton must be sick again. It's a little code. Neither of us likes to upset Ellen. Tomorrow is the Feast of the Epiphany. A Jewish girl, a visit from royalty. Gifts.
> "He says fine." She's pleased. "I think it's a valuable connection for you."
> "You may be right."

The playfulness of the passage lies in the unresolved contrast of Ellen's secular reading of the signals and More's confident knowledge that the call is indeed eucharistic in nature. It seems clear, too, that Fr. Smith would like to draw More also into the work of the hospice, which serves the neediest of their society's needy: malformed infants and victims of AIDS and Alzheimer's disease. With a caution typical of Percy's fictional characters, More casts his anticipation of the possibility of an epiphany in his life in the subjunctive mood: "You *may be* right." This is a caution that serves the timidity of More's faith well, and that challenges our own reluctance to serve others, the least of Jesus' brethren, especially those most obviously in greatest need within reach.

I consider these novels by O'Connor and Percy as stories of the Savior, when they might more appropriately, as we shall see, be read as stories of the Lifegiver—not because they portray savior figures as such, but rather because they focus indirectly on the effects of Jesus' redemptive mission on our lives through eucharistic imagery and settings—the memorial invitation to sacrifice our whole lives, body and blood, talents and energy for the sake of others.

Resurrection:
Images of Liberation

Recording the central mystery of our faith—the Resurrection—the Evangelists challenge us with the image of the empty tomb and the announcement, "He is risen—he is not here!" Artists throughout the history of Christianity have generally chosen more reassuring symbols: the phoenix rising resplendent from its ashes, the peacock (originally associated with immortality), and the butterfly bursting from its cocoon. In conquering death, Jesus proclaims the joyous paradox of the Good News of our salvation: if we die to self, we live in him. It is this paradoxical conjunction of self-sacrifice and liberation that we see made flesh in the best stories of the Savior. Those that come closest to the fullness of Christian belief are almost always stories of liberation, the literary and cinematic analogue of renewal, rebirth, even resurrection.

Elia Kazan's *On the Waterfront*, a stirring film about justice in the workplace and liberation from oppression, is one of those obvious stories of the Savior that addresses our understanding of the meaning of the Resurrection for our lives. Budd Schulberg, the screenwriter, had been attracted by the account of Fr. John Corridan's efforts to fight corruption in the New York longshoremen's unions in the early 1950s; a series of articles on waterfront crime, written by Malcolm Johnson, provided the setting for the story as well as the patterns of conflict and resolution. Elia Kazan, who had only recently cooperated with the House Un-American Activities Committee by "naming names" (but none that had not already been named) of Hollywood communist sympathizers, was drawn, perhaps in self-justification, toward presenting the story of a justified informer. As attitudes in Hollywood toward HUAC informers hardened in the ensuing decades, Kazan was unofficially but effectively shunned by the Motion Picture Academy until 1999 when, in his nineties, he was belatedly awarded a much-deserved Oscar for his lifetime achievement in film, even though some in the audience self-righteously refused to applaud the honor.

Out of the collaboration of Schulberg and Kazan came the tense dramatic story of Terry Malloy, the exfighter, played so convincingly by Marlon Brando, whose conscience awakens to the stark reality of union corruption when the brutal tactics of the union boss Johnny Friendly touch his life. His subsequent testimony before the New York Crime Commission results in Friendly's exposure and expulsion from union leadership. Although Terry does not die in the typical pattern of the Savior, he is beaten to a pulp in his physical confrontation with Friendly and his "goons." We nonetheless experience a kind of resurrection, as the film builds to a climax, when Terry rises from a pool of blood to lead the oppressed dockworkers victoriously up the gangplank to the door of the warehouse. Banded together, they all get work even though the ousted boss had sworn Terry would never again be hired.

Graham Greene's powerful novel *The Power and the Glory*, originally published in the United States as *The Labyrinthine Ways*, presents one of fiction's most compelling and unique savior stories. Set in Mexico early in the century during the period of the Church's suppression, it tells the story of a "whiskey priest" who rises above his doubts about his faith and the weakness of his flesh and, while fulfilling the duties expected of him as a priest, is apprehended and executed, dying a martyr's death. There is no doubt in the novel that his faith has finally saved him. *The Fugitive*, John Ford's adaptation of Greene, sanitizes the priest's life, perhaps in deference to his devout immigrant Irish Catholic sensibility, certainly in anticipation of industry censorship. At any rate, his "padre," played by Henry Fonda, feels that he has been unfaithful to his priesthood because he pridefully claims to have been the last priest in the film's nameless land of persecution south of the border, when in reality he knows himself to have been a coward and fled. Finally, he is betrayed by a mestizo Judas, who pursues him out of the country, coaxing him back under false pretenses to give the last sacraments to a dying American criminal. The film is quite explicit in its resurrection imagery; after the padre's execution as a common criminal, and presumably because of the courage of his sacrifice, a new priest, facing persecution and possible execution, appears at the door of the church to minister to the padre's former flock—death has yielded new life.

Ford's more faithful adaptation of John Steinbeck's *The Grapes of Wrath*, in part because it involves less explicitly religious material, provides us, I feel, with cinema's purest instance of a fictional savior: the parallels of Jim Casy's life to the gospel narrative are classic in simplicity. Jim Casy is a failed preacher, yet a man with a vision. His initials fit his function perfectly. As played by John Carradine, whose initials were also ideal for the part, Casy has a gaunt, determined, otherworldly look. The story follows the Joads as they take Route 66 west from the Oklahoma dust bowl with Casy along, in search of the promised land of work in California, but all that is left for them to pick when they arrive are "the grapes of wrath." In the film's climactic sequence, Casy urges workers to organize in opposition to the landowners. Deputies raid their hidden encampment; one kills Casy and is killed in turn by Tom Joad, who then becomes a fugitive from justice, hidden by his family. In the classic pattern of the Christ-figure, Casy's death liberates Tom from bondage to his family, but more importantly it frees him to serve the needy everywhere by working to expel society's demon of economic exploitation.

The expatriate Czech Milos Forman, ironically one of the keenest observers of the American scene, achieved his greatest success as director, in my estimation, with his adaptation of Ken Kesey's novel *One Flew Over the Cuckoo's Nest*. Although there are variations in the way this unique drama of liberation is played out in novel and film, the structure of both works is basically the same: Randle Patrick McMurphy is committed to a mental hospital, *laughing*, challenges the oppressive system, is destroyed by it, but lives on in his disciple, Chief Broom. The theme of liberating laughter, which we simply observe in the film, is clearly enunciated in the novel. In a wonderful mixture of images, McMurphy tells Cheswick: "Man, when you lose your laugh you lose your *footing*." The Christmas party, in both novel and film, is proof that even "chronics" can finally be coaxed into laughter. The film, of course, ends with an electrifying shot of Taber's insane laugh of approval at the chief's escape, that awakens the dead left on the ward.

In both novel and film, McMurphy becomes effective as a liberator only when he turns away from a frontal assault on Nurse Ratched and directs his attention toward the needs of his fellow inmates. The motivation for his transformation is the same in both works—namely, the discovery that he is not in control of his fate, even though the occasion for the discovery is different. In the novel, Nurse Ratched herself provides the threat when she turns off the TV set McMurphy has turned on, thinking he has won the vote about watching the world-series game. "Mr. McMurphy, I'm *warning* you!" she shrieks. "You're committed, you realize. You are . . . under the *jurisdiction* of me . . . the staff. . . . Under jurisdiction and *control*—." In the film, ever less direct than the novel, McMurphy finds this out from Washington during water therapy, when he tells the black aide he will settle scores with him as soon as he serves his time and gets out. Washington taunts him, saying, "You're going to stay with us till we let you go."

The final confrontation between McMurphy and Nurse Ratched is given a more explicit sexual reading in the novel than in the film, but almost everything in the novel is drawn in bold, expressionistic strokes by comparison. In the film, McMurphy lunges for Nurse Ratched's throat, trying to strangle her, and falls on top of her, but is knocked unconscious by an aide. The novel portrays Nurse Ratched as hiding the woman inside of her stiff nurse's uniform, her professional armor, but as a result of McMurphy's assault, in which he rips open her uniform exposing her breasts, with nipples swollen, she will never again be able to conceal her womanhood. In a variety of ways, the novel makes it clearer than the film that McMurphy has had a lasting effect on Nurse Ratched herself. However minimal a victory it is, it is nonetheless McMurphy's victory; it is both his dying and his rising from the dead. It even eclipses Chief Broom's liberation as victory because, in transforming Nurse Ratched, he has reformed the impersonal institution itself.

On the other hand, the chief's liberation from the ward—not McMurphy's victory over Ratched—is the film's climactic moment; it is also, in my estimation, cinema's most memorable image of resurrection. In Forman's presentation, the chief is not only in control of his actions and his plans, but also fully aware of the source of his strength. And the dialogue is entirely between the chief and the speechless, lobotomized McMurphy. As soon as the nurses and orderlies leave the ward for the night, the chief gets up and dresses, obviously ready to leave. Bending over McMurphy, he says, "Mac, they said you'd escaped. I knew you wouldn't do it without me." Then raising McMurphy to a sitting position, he sees the scars on his forehead, and mutters with recognition, "Oh, no!" As his realization deepens, he insists, "I'm not going without you, Mac. I wouldn't leave you here this way," and our only reasonable expectation at this point is that the chief will somehow carry McMurphy's body away. Instead, letting the inert body down on the bed, he tells McMurphy, "You're coming with me. Let's go." With the help of a pillow, he proceeds to press out whatever breath remains in McMurphy's body. True to his Native American spirituality, he knows that McMurphy's inert body is no longer a suitable shrine for his irrepressible spirit. McMurphy will indeed go with him; more accurately, he will go with McMurphy's spirit. The film's lasting image of resurrection results from Forman's brilliant jump cut, as we move abruptly from inside the confining ward, where the chief lunges at the window with the control panel, to the outside—to see both the panel and the chief explode through the window frame behind shattered glass and splintered wood, a piece of the wooden frame swinging back and forth like a winding sheet left hanging in the breeze at the opening of the tomb.

The chief's escape is, of course, a stunning image of liberation. But from whom, or what? The most plausible answer would seem to be American Puritanism, in all its forms, but especially those structures of national repression, represented in the novel by America-the-Combine, that are impersonal, mechanical, sexless, and inhuman. The film, less explicit about the sources of our collective woes, suggests that institutions themselves, encrusted with regulations and prohibitions, and those who control them—mostly to protect themselves and their power—have become our universal oppressors, of mind and body.

John Schlesinger's adaptation of James Leo Herlihy's novel *Midnight Cowboy* is a tribute to the liberating power of fraternal love in the midst of, and despite, the hazards of the impersonal city. Joe Buck leaves rural Texas for New York City expecting to strike it rich as a stud. Everything along the way—billboards, neon signs, radio talk-shows, TV—seems humorously to support his naive ambition; later the same media will comment ironically on the absurdity of his sexual odyssey. Joe luckily encounters Ratso Rizzo, a streetwise urban con man. Ratso's deformed and consumptive body is the visual reversal of Joe's attractive though presumptuous appearance. A deep bond of friendship develops slowly but surely between the two men. Just as Joe seems finally at a chic party to make a successful sexual contact through Sylvia, he abandons his empty ambitions in order to take Ratso south, in hope that the warm climate will cure his illness, not realizing how close Ratso is to death.

Touching imagery of rebirth confirms the transforming power of their love and the sacrifice it has prompted. Joe finally calls Ratso "Rico" as he has always wanted, and as they approach Miami, Joe discards his cowboy outfit and buys them both new shirts. Rico's, the last one available with brightly painted palm trees on it, becomes a joyous shroud for his passage through death; Joe's plain shirt suggests the dawn for him of a more realistic new start in life. Jon Voight and Dustin Hoffman are ideally cast as Joe and Ratso respectively; visually they are perfect complements. In the typical pattern of buddy films, it is the weaker partner who effects the salvation of the stronger. This is a paradox, of course, that is appropriately similar to St. Paul's theology of the cross: "Divine folly is wiser than the wisdom of man, and divine weakness stronger than man's strength" (1 Corinthians 1:25).

Where in this context of faith nourished by fiction does one place Steven Spielberg's *E.T.: The Extraterrestrial*? Like *Close Encounters of the Third Kind*, which we have already discussed, *E.T.* is more than a film about extraordinary space phenomena. Spielberg is an artist whose imagination is deeply rooted in the Bible as well as in the classic myths of our Western heritage. Since there is convincing evidence that the film's core concern is love's capacity to save and to renew, it seems appropriate to consider it a savior story. The spaceship that E.T. was traveling on is forced suddenly to leave its southern California landing site because of the approach of curious, if not hostile humans. E.T. is accidentally left behind and becomes himself the sole object of the hunt. Eluding his captors, he is befriended by a little boy named Elliott, whose younger sister and older brother join him in the conspiracy to protect the visitor from outer space. Eavesdropping scientists are never too far away from the suburban home that shelters him.

Because E.T. has superior intelligence and even magical powers by earth's standards, he has been considered by some religious commentators to be an angelic visitor. He heals cuts with the touch of his finger, brings a dying plant back to full bloom, makes bicycles fly simply by concentrating, and learns enough of the earthlings' language to tell Elliott that he wants to "phone home." He also seems capable, for a time, of entering into Elliott's consciousness so that each feels what the other feels. Although analogies to angelic powers are interesting, the ending of the story is more consonant with our understanding of stories of the Savior.

Out in the woods where Elliott and E.T. deploy the makeshift communications device that the latter builds to signal his spaceship, the two youths become separated. Apparently because he is without Elliott's special care, E.T. languishes; he has also perhaps been too long deprived of his own environment. Near death, E.T. becomes the prey of invading scientists, protected from contamination by spacesuits, able to wait no longer to conduct their experiments. Spielberg makes it clear that science has no place in the sphere of the interpersonal. Appallingly ashen, E.T. dies—or at least is pronounced dead by our limited human instruments—but is brought back to life by Elliott's protestation of love, a capacity that E.T. has awakened in him. Despite the best efforts of science and the law, the children help E.T. reach the designated rendezvous with his spaceship. And before he "ascends" into the heavens, he assures the saddened Elliott that he is not really leaving him, as he touches Elliott's forehead, saying, "I will be here!" Love conquers death, or at least its appearance, and mutual love transcends society's oppressive forces.

Life between Two Comings: Parables of Judgment

The stories of the Savior that we have appealed to thus far provide us with literary and cinematic analogues of the heart of the paschal mystery: the passion, death, and resurrection of Jesus. Because the substance of the meaning of our salvation is reflected in those articles of the creed, it would have been artificial, as I noted in the Introduction, to have looked for fictional equivalents for each of the creed's individual propositions related to the Second Person of the Trinity, that make up the second and by far the longest part of the Apostles' Creed. Nonetheless, it seems appropriate in concluding this part to offer some specific reflections on the meaning of those other articles for our lives today—lived as they are, happily, between two comings.

First of all, we affirm our faith in the Second Person of the Trinity by confessing Jesus Christ as God's only Son and our Lord. What unites us as Christians is our belief that God so loved us that he became man in order to save us. Heaven and earth, the divine and the human, come together in perfect harmony in the person of Jesus. God our Father and Creator is no longer remote from us. Indeed, through the Incarnation, the invisible God became fully visible in the presence of Jesus, his Son. As we read in the Gospel of John, Jesus himself reassured his apostles after the Last Supper, "He who has seen me has seen the Father" (John 14:9). The same Evangelist, appealing to the account of creation in Genesis 1 and thus to the image of a God who utters the creative word, actually begins his Gospel with this startling revelation: The Word that is God speaking has become man.

As a consequence of our belief in the Incarnation of the Word, we must constantly be alert to the fact that we live in a world that is forever altered by the presence of grace. Grace is obviously offered to us through the sacraments of the Church, most of which as a matter of fact employ material things: water, oil, bread, wine. The embodiment of grace does not, of course, stop there. As a result of the Incarnation, "everything is grace," Andrew Greeley insists, or, as I prefer to put it, "Grace is everywhere, and everything is potentially grace." Expressing it yet another way, Richard McBrien writes, "The Catholic vision sees God in and through all things: other people, communities, movements, events, places, objects, the world at large, the whole cosmos. The visible, the tangible, the finite, the historical—all these are actual or potential carriers of the divine presence" (*Catholicism*).

The two mysteries that introduce the creed's brief history of God among us—the Annunciation and the virgin birth—offer specific biblical images for our belief in this radically new union of the divine and the human. The child that Mary gives birth to comes into the world through God's miraculous intervention. The only appropriate response to the revelation of God's compassionate plan for our salvation, as Mary's example demonstrates to us, is unconditional self-surrender. In her acceptance of God's invitation to be the mother of his Son, we discover the peace that comes from total submission to God's will even if it means—and it invariably does—accepting the passion as well. If, with Mary, our souls magnify the Lord and we confidently say, "Let it be," inner peace will surely be ours too, but a peace, we know now in the hindsight of belief, that comes only through suffering.

What, though, are we to make of the creed's affirmation—"he descended to the dead"—that immediately follows our confession of Jesus' burial? The phrase "to the dead" replaces "into hell" in contemporary versions of the Apostles' Creed, the better perhaps to reflect the Church's traditional explanation of this article, namely, that Jesus, between his burial and resurrection, liberated the souls of the just from limbo, who were awaiting the time of their salvation. "In the spirit," we read in the First Letter of Peter, "he went and made his proclamation to the imprisoned spirits" (3:19). Even with this clarification, the relevance of this article for our lives today may be elusive. The image of the new translation—"to the dead"—seems at least to emphasize our belief that death, which awaits us all, was an experience that Jesus as man had in its fullness. As a result, everything we associate with death—the loneliness, isolation, desolation, and even abandonment—he has sanctified for each of us. No aspect of death then can retain its sting.

The last articles of the creed's central part pertain to Jesus' exaltation. At the heart of faith in his ascension lies our awareness that in this period prior to Jesus's second coming, we cannot count upon the palpable, personal presence that his disciples and followers enjoyed. We are nonetheless expected to be about our Father's business, and not be idle gazers at the heavens. Like the apostles, we must give witness to Jesus "to the ends of the earth." We must accept the task of discipleship implicit in his leave-taking and commission to the apostles.

"Sitting at the right hand of the Father" is the creed's image for what the New Testament describes both as Jesus' glorification (see John 17) and as his exaltation (see Philippians 2:5–11)—an image nonetheless that recapitulates the bold, initial confession in this part of the creed of Jesus as "our Lord." The mystery we profess here is of a single theological fabric with Jesus' death and resurrection. *Because* Jesus humbled himself, God has exalted him and given him the name that is above every name, his own name: Lord. Whatever we accomplish, we do in and through his divine name.

Although our belief in Jesus' second coming is expressed in the creed in terms of his judging the living and the dead, Scripture makes it abundantly clear that we have already been judged by his first coming. In John's Gospel, Jesus proclaims, "It is for judgment that I have come into this world—to give sight to the sightless and to make blind those who see" (9:39). Indeed, as we have seen, professing faith in the redemptive power of Jesus' love is an implicit judgment of our selfishness, our infidelity, our despair. To the extent that we have failed to love one another as he has loved us, we have failed to live the faith that we profess. Matthew's Gospel provides us perhaps with the definitive story of the Savior—the great parable of judgment (see 25:31–46)—which shows us how the Son of Man, when he comes in glory, will exalt those who have cared for the least of his brethren. If we have welcomed strangers, fed the hungry, given drink to the thirsty, clothed the naked, visited the sick and prisoners, we have actually comforted the Son of Man himself and shall be named the "blessed" of his Father. This is, of course, comforting knowledge; putting it into practice, we know from experience, is another matter altogether. Our efforts to live and act accordingly, though, will be the measure of our acceptance of Jesus' redemptive grace.

There is a sense of course in which all great fiction judges our lives; this is specifically true of certain contemporary literary and cinematic parables of judgment. *To Kill a Mockingbird*, both Harper Lee's Pulitzer

Prize novel about growing up in a small Alabama town in the 1930s and Robert Mulligan's excellent film adaptation, is a double-edged story of the Savior. It not only appeals indirectly, but nonetheless clearly, to Matthew's parable of the final judgment, but also presents its own unique image of the Savior. Although told as a remembrance, the story is anything but nostalgic. It is about seeing through others' eyes until we can see for ourselves—and about remembering to be grateful for the way we are taught by our elders early on to read the world. For Scout and her slightly older brother, Jem, it is their wise, generous, and gentle lawyer father, Atticus Finch (one of Gregory Peck's great film roles), who shares with them, as the occasion warrants, the kinds of practical insights that we need in order to live with compassion. Atticus tells his daughter, "If you can learn a simple trick, Scout, you'll get along a lot better with all kinds of folks. You never really understand a person until you consider things from his point of view—until you climb into his skin and walk around in it." Two narrative strands are carefully interwoven: the children's determination to expose the mystery of their retarded neighbor, Boo Radley, and Atticus's doomed defense of a black man falsely accused of rape. Atticus's philosophy and his devotion to racial justice are direct appeals to gospel values; his defense of Robinson is a clear illustration of what the parable means about caring for our least brethren. Boo Radley, although a minor character, is the true savior figure in the story; his portrayal in the film is the memorable screen debut of the great character actor Robert Duvall. On Halloween night, when Bob Ewell tries to avenge Atticus's defense of Robinson by harming his children, Boo saves the children's lives—and, in reasonable gratitude, they want to tell everyone the source of their good fortune. But, Scout rightly concludes, if it is "a sin to kill a mockingbird" because all they do is sing pretty songs, then it would be like killing a mockingbird to deprive reclusive Boo Radley of his privacy by telling everyone of his heroism. In being sensitive to Boo Radley's need to stay to himself, they are caring in effect for the Son of Man.

The most extraordinary indictment of modern society ever brought to the screen, though, is surely Federico Fellini's *La Dolce Vita*. Some, myself included, consider it one of the greatest cinematic creations of the religious imagination. There is no savior figure as such in the film—only the suggestion at the end of an angelic messenger, although perhaps of the sort that we find in the patriarchal narratives of Genesis, messengers who are really the incarnate presence of Yahweh. Nonetheless, it has such a stunning opening sequence, one of cinema's most memorable, that it is hard not to think of it as a story of the Savior. In fact, *La Dolce Vita*'s opening *and* closing sequences provide a striking biblical framework for judgment— of a world that, despite Jesus' coming into it, seems immune to grace.

As the film begins, a statue of Christ the Laborer is being carried by helicopter to the pope across the Roman skyline, passing over the ruins of the San Felice aqueduct, then over modern high-rise apartment buildings, before pausing majestically over the great dome of St. Peter's, as the bells of the basilica toll triumphantly. The succession of images suggests that the Son of Man has come to judge all ages and peoples—past *and* present, the secular *and* the sacred. The film ends on a beach near Rome where an immense, amorphous fish has been dragged out of the sea and stares with dead, accusing eye at the curious bystanders. We can find an adequate reference for this imagery only in the Book of Revelation when, after the blast of the seventh trumpet, the appalling beast from the sea appears that blasphemes God and his dwelling place (see 13:1). Between these framing images of judgment, the events of the film transpire in eight nights and nine mornings, suggesting that Fellini complemented his biblical imagery with a structure taken from the first part of Italy's greatest religious epic, Dante's *Inferno*—namely, the nine circles of judgment in hell.

Each day offers up a different aspect of contemporary society for judgment, with the nights presenting opportunities that the dawns find us grossly incapable of accepting. Thus on nine successive days, the Eternal City of Rome becomes Dante's City of Dis. In the person of Marcello, a Roman newspaperman, who is Fellini's modern "everyman," we are offered wealth, stardom, religion, art, family, tradition, love, sensual oblivion, and even grace—the last in the form of a beautiful young girl whom Marcello calls his "Umbrian angel." Salvation comes to us, Fellini suggests, in the form of different opportunities for creativity and new life. If we do not answer, he insists, it is not because the invitation is no longer made, but rather because our sensitivity to the voice of mystery has been deadened by the clamor of the flesh.

Woody Allen's *Crimes and Misdemeanors* presents the dilemma of a man who discovers, as should be obvious, that for the time being at least— that is to say, while history endures—God apparently remains silent about our crimes as well as our misdemeanors. The film's hero, if he can in any sense be called that, is amazed as time goes by to discover that God not only fails to chastise him for having his mistress murdered, but also seems to permit him, however uneasily, to continue to thrive. Allen, perhaps unknowingly, offers here a variation on another parable of judgment of

Matthew's: Jesus' likening the Kingdom of God to a field in which the wheat and the weeds are allowed to grow together till harvest (see 13:24–30).

Reflecting on the meaning for our lives of Jesus' second coming reminds us that, in reality if not in the liturgy, our whole Christian life is lived in Advent. The major difference between the second and the first is that now we know what to expect and, more pointedly, what is expected of us. Precisely when Jesus comes is, though, as obscured now as it was then. In terms of the fiction we have been exploring, there is no better source for an appreciation of Christian "waiting" than in Flannery O'Connor's stories, since they are all about characters, not unlike ourselves, who either forget that they are waiting or experience something quite different from what they expected or wanted.

We have already considered "A Good Man Is Hard to Find" as a story of the Creator, specifically of stewardship limited by mortality. Insofar as its theme of tragic judgment centers upon the grandmother's failure to recognize her least brethren and reminds us also that we know not the day or the hour, it is also a story of the Savior. O'Connor's other great short stories—especially "Revelation," "The Artificial Nigger," and "Good Country People"—will reward a reading in this context. None of these stories has the apocalyptic ending of "A Good Man Is Hard to Find," but each is nonetheless about being ready for judgment when it comes; and in the sacramental world that O'Connor, like her fellow southerner Walker Percy, is so adept at portraying, judgment is invariably embodied in everyday events and things.

Joy, the protagonist of "Good Country People," is a highly educated woman of thirty-two, in fact a Ph.D. in philosophy, who apparently believes that "Nothing" is at the heart of reality, perhaps as a subconscious reaction to having lost a leg in a hunting accident when she was ten. She even changes her name to Hulga because it sounds ugly enough to subvert her mother's choice of Joy. Despite her haughty self-confidence, Hulga eventually succumbs to the wiles of an uneducated country con artist, selling Bibles, whom she had hoped to "convert" to her way of looking at things. Left stranded by him without her glasses and the artificial leg that she protected as if it were her soul, she is seared by the judgment of her demonic intellectual inferior, who tells her simply, "You ain't so smart. I been believing in nothing ever since I was born!"

In "The Artificial Nigger," Mr. Head and his grandson, Nelson, acting as if they were Pride and Son of Pride in a rural Georgia version of *Everyman*, take a day's trip into Atlanta because Mr. Head wants Nelson to see what "the city" is really like so that he will be content to stay at home in the country. At the end of a long day, when the old man himself gets lost in the bowels of the city trying to find his way back to the train station, like a confused Virgil leading Dante out of hell, and has to admit his ignorance to Nelson, he discovers his fallen condition, typified by his racist attitudes, reflected in a disfigured lawn statue that they encounter on the road. Needing redemption, Mr. Head experiences the action of mercy in the presence of "the artificial nigger" that lends the story its regionally precise, but nonetheless potentially offensive name.

Ruby Turpin in "Revelation," whose shocking indictment by Mary Grace I mentioned in the introduction—"Go back to hell where you came from, you old wart hog"—finally acknowledges herself judged by God, even though she mistakenly likens herself to Job (he had done nothing to deserve the ills that befell him). Ruby is forced by the assault of the emotionally disturbed college student, with the ironically appropriate name, to reconsider her foolish conviction, pompously proclaimed in a doctor's waiting room, that she knows how humans are ranked in the eyes of God— she and her husband coming in second only to those who had a little more money and property than they had. Thanks to the grace that Mary Grace's calling her a hog (and thus "unclean") turns out to be, Ruby grows gradually but surely into the knowledge that in the current dispensation, the first shall be last and the last first.

If we were to live each moment as if it were our last, we would be ready for judgment and, of course, the world would be a far better place. We would then consciously pray that when our time comes, our virtues will light the way—like so many lamps kept trimmed through Jesus' grace, in anticipation of his coming. As O'Connor's "A Good Man Is Hard to Find" reminds us, to live in Advent is to live "under the gun."

I believe in the Holy Spirit,
the holy catholic church, the communion of saints,
the forgiveness of sins,
the resurrection of the body and life everlasting.
Amen.

I believe, to be sure, that any man who reaches Heaven will find that what he abandoned (even in plucking out his right eye) was precisely nothing: that the kernel of what he was really seeking even in his most depraved wishes will be there, beyond expectation, waiting for him in the "high countries." In that sense it will be true for those who have completed the journey (and for no others) to say that good is everything and Heaven is everywhere. But we, at this end of the road, must not try to anticipate that retrospective vision. If we do, we are likely to embrace the false and disastrous converse and fancy that everything is good and everywhere is Heaven.

But what, you ask, of earth? Earth, I think, will not be found by anyone to be in the end a very distinct place. I think earth, if chosen instead of Heaven, will turn out to have been, all along, only a region in Hell: and earth, if put second to Heaven, to have been from the beginning a part of Heaven itself.

—C. S. Lewis, *The Great Divorce*

Stories of the Lifegiver

In Flannery O'Connor's short story "The Enduring Chill," a failed young artist named Asbury returns home to die, or so he thinks. When O'Connor describes his conviction that death will come to him "as a justification, as a gift from life," she is consciously using language associated with the Holy Spirit as well as foreshadowing the story's final revelation. Even though the image of the title is ironically worlds apart from the affirmative metaphors that the New Testament uses for the gifts of the Spirit, O'Connor has nonetheless given us one of modern fiction's finest stories of the Lifegiver.

Death seems to be the only thing Asbury, with extreme self-pity, is capable of taking seriously, aside from the fact that he wants his dying to be a lesson to his mother. To offend her traditional beliefs, he asks to see the nearby Jesuit priest, hoping that the local priest will be "a trifle more worldly perhaps, a trifle more cynical" than Ignatius Vogle, the sophisticated young Jesuit he had met in New York. Instead, he is visited by Fr. Finn, "a massive old man," deaf in one ear and blind in one eye, who is anything but sophisticated. The priest asks whether Asbury has any "trouble with purity," whether he says his morning and night prayers and knows his catechism. Finally, in exasperation at Asbury's agnostic answers, Fr. Finn tells him bluntly that he had better ask God "to send the Holy Ghost," to which Asbury responds furiously, "The Holy Ghost is the last thing I'm looking for." The priest answers simply, "He may be the last thing you get."

When Asbury discovers that he is not dying, but has undulant fever caused by his stupidity in drinking unpasteurized milk, he is left sadly to himself and his own devices, confined to bed in the presence of a "fierce bird with spread wings, . . . an icicle crosswise in its beak," formed by water stains on the ceiling. The bird often gave, we are told, the illusion of being in motion and about to descend. As the story ends, the "purifying terror" of its descent coincides with the recurring waves of the chill that grips Asbury's body. Father Finn's prophetic judgment has come to literal fulfillment, as well as Fr. Vogle's more cautious assertion, at a party Asbury had attended, that "there is . . . a real probability of the New Man, assisted, of course, . . . by the Third Person of the Trinity." The last thing Asbury wanted is, providentially for him, the last thing he gets: the steady descent of the chastening Spirit "emblazoned in ice instead of fire."

Among other things, the story invites us, like Asbury, to heed the icy truth about ourselves, that being left to our own devices is a fate worse than death. On another level, and one closer to the truth of stories of the Lifegiver, it reminds us that grace is mediated to us through others and through commonplace events—for Asbury, through Fr. Finn and the stain on his ceiling that he will not be able to avoid seeing. If Asbury's realization that he has caused his illness and has no one to blame but himself for "the enduring chill" that he will experience is indeed the beginning of his conversion, the story suggests that the way to repentance begins with submission to the always unexpected, often shattering graces of everyday events.

Stories of the Lifegiver answer Huston Smith's third fundamental religious question with the resounding affirmation that salvation comes with and through others; that is to say, in community, however limited.

Gifts of the Spirit:
Living with and through Others

Because references to the *lifegiving* function of the Holy Spirit pervade the Bible, it is appropriately, as I have noted, the image that is used in the Nicene Creed to distinguish the Spirit from Father and Son. In Genesis the Spirit of God hovers over the waters, ready to breathe life into creation (see Genesis 1:1). The infancy narratives in the Gospels of Matthew and Luke are explicit about the Holy Spirit's role in Mary's virginal conception, thus giving life to the New Adam, the new creation (see Matthew 1:20; Luke 1:34–35). The Spirit, in sustaining Jesus through the two events that immediately precede his public ministry, gives life as it were to his mission of salvation. When Jesus is baptized by John in the Jordan, the Spirit descends upon him "like a dove" (see Mark 1:10, Matthew 3:16, Luke 3:22); and it is the Spirit who leads Jesus into the wilderness, where he is tempted by the devil (see Matthew 4:1, Luke 4:1–2).

According to the Gospel of John, on the last day of the Feast of the Tabernacles, Jesus cries aloud: "If anyone is thirsty let him come to me; whoever believes in me, let him drink." Then the Evangelist explains: "As scripture says, 'Streams of living water shall flow out from within him.' He was speaking of the Spirit which believers in him would receive later; for the Spirit had not yet been given, because Jesus had not yet been glorified" (John 7:37–39). It is St. Paul, though, in his First Letter to the Corinthians, who provides us with the most striking equation of Jesus, the Spirit, and life. Referring to the "spiritual" body of the risen Christ as opposed to the "animal" body of Jesus' weakness and humiliation, he adds: "It is in this sense that scripture says, 'The first man, Adam, became an animate being,' whereas the last Adam has become a life-giving spirit" (1 Corinthians 15:45). Saint Paul not only asserts the Spirit's equality with Jesus, but also reaffirms his life-giving role.

In writing about the gifts of the Spirit, St. Paul gives us a variety of specific ways that we can judge the presence of his life-giving grace. To the Galatians, he writes: "The harvest of the Spirit is love, joy, peace, patience, kindness, goodness, fidelity, gentleness and self-control" (5:22). For the Colossians, he adds the virtues of "compassion" and "humility" (3:12). Tradition settled finally on *seven* gifts of the Holy Spirit (wisdom, understanding, counsel, fortitude, knowledge, piety, and fear of the Lord), not in any sense to limit the action of grace, but rather by use of the symbolic number to indicate the fullness and perfection of the Spirit's gifts.

The First Letter to the Corinthians, chapters 12–14, presents St. Paul's richest instruction about the gifts of the Spirit. There are many gifts, he writes, but only one Spirit. Some gifts are community functions given to particular individuals within the body of Christ—such as apostles, prophets, teachers, miracle-workers, healers, speakers in tongues, and interpreters of tongues. Others are personal qualities that each of us, presumably, is offered for the sake of the whole. But the virtues that "last for ever," Paul tells the Corinthians, are faith, hope, and love, love being "the greatest of them all." He explains in even greater detail:

> Love is patient; love is kind and envies no one. Love is never boastful, nor conceited, nor rude; never selfish, not quick to take offence. Love keeps no score of wrongs; does not gloat over other men's sins, but delights in the truth. There is nothing love cannot face; there is no limit to its faith, its hope, and its endurance. Love will never come to an end.

This extraordinary passage is especially instructive in this context because it provides particular images for the action of the Spirit seeking to transform our lives from within, that we will find reflected in stories of the

Lifegiver. That transforming power of the Spirit that would affect every aspect of our lives, though given a plenitude of names in Scripture, came simply in tradition to be called *grace*. Grace is both the action of the Spirit and its effect upon our lives.

Some stories of the Lifegiver explicitly announce their theme in words synonymous with gifts of the Spirit. Frank Capra's renowned film *It's a Wonderful Life* is perhaps cinema's most notable analogue of the Spirit's distinctive gift. Angels figure prominently in the drama that unfolds, but to the eyes of faith, they represent the Spirit whom Jesus has sent to show us "the life" as well as to direct us in living that life. Even in the world of the film, the angel Clarence is clearly a messenger under the direction of a higher heavenly power referred to simply as "Sir." Despite its Christmas setting, though, there is a dark side to the film inasmuch as George Bailey, memorably played by Jimmy Stewart, is struggling within himself to reconcile his impulse to help others with his desire for adventure and wealth. And because of his deep dissatisfaction with the direction he perceives his life is taking, he contemplates taking his own life.

As the story unfolds, George is able—through Clarence's help—to see what the town of Bedford Falls would have been like if he had not lived. We all, if we would attend to our inspirations, make a difference, as George Bailey discovers, especially if we live with generosity and with the assurance of God's love for us. The film is full of reminders of its theme, in a way perhaps that by today's standards may seem too obvious, yet each is integral to the story and to the time in which it is set. The motto under the portrait of George's father in the office of the building and loan is: "All you can take with you is that which you've given away." And the inscription that Clarence leaves for George in the copy of *The Adventures of Tom Sawyer* is "Remember no man is a failure who has friends."

The fact of the matter is that many of Frank Capra's films were explicitly intended for our faith's nourishment, and his other perennial favorites are well worth viewing as stories of the Lifegiver—especially *Mr. Deeds Goes to Town*, *You Can't Take It With You*, and *Mr. Smith Goes to Washington*. Like John Ford, Capra was born to an immigrant Catholic family. Throughout his career in Hollywood, which spanned the major studio years of the film industry, he seemed totally faithful in his filmmaking to the religious values he had learned as a youth. In his autobiography, Capra boldly proclaims, "My films must let every man, woman, and child know that God loves them, and that I love them, and that peace and salvation will become a reality only when they learn to love each other." Just because he wanted to achieve this effect in his films does not, of course, automatically mean that he did, but their continued inspiration of viewers seems to attest to the fact that his ennobling vision must be evident in them.

Two films with central appeals to life, its sources, and related values I mention here briefly on the assumption that everyone will be familiar with them—Morton DaCosta's *Auntie Mame* and George Lucas' *Star Wars*—but strongly recommend their reviewing in this context. In *Auntie Mame*—one of the most enjoyable film comedies ever made mainly because of Rosalind Russell's singular performance in the title role—the invitation to live is the film's central message and the heart of the flamboyant title character's philosophy of life. Mame Dennis impatiently instructs her timorous secretary: "Live, live, live! Life is a banquet, Agnes, and most poor fools are starving to death." Those who starve are the people who fail to take responsibility for their own lives or, more pointedly, who are such snobs that they are afraid they will be contaminated by life's rich diversity of opportunities.

Star Wars, the first and arguably still the best of George Lucas' cycle of space films, is, like *Auntie Mame*, about education to those values that are at the core of genuine human existence. When Ben Obi-Wan Kenobi tells Luke Skywaker, "The Force be with you!" he is urging him to be united with the transcendent source of life that enables him to conquer agents of death and destruction. Although many commentators have taken the Force to be a direct reference to the Spirit, it is clear from its description that it is a physical power field; of course, the physical is frequently emblematic of the realm of the Spirit.

One of the particular gifts of the Spirit that has figured notably in film is healing as a source of life. Richard Pearce's *Leap of Faith*, that supports also our sense of life's purposeful flow of events, deserves consideration principally as a story of the Lifegiver, I think, because its setting is a community of faith brought together, ironically enough, by a cynical showman masking as a traveling preacher. Unlike Sinclair Lewis's *Elmer Gantry*, the classic tale of a hypocritical revivalist in the midst of apparent believers who is exposed as a sinner, *Leap of Faith* features a con artist who does not believe a thing that he preaches and who uses the best computerized communications technology to drain the pocketbooks of innocent believers.

Jonas Nigthengale, played to perfection by Steve Martin, is quite simply a fraud—and his traveling troupe seems to know it and accept it. When they are forced by mechanical problems with one of their trucks to stay four days in a small Kansas town, Jones decides to pitch his tent and make whatever money he can. Drought has plagued this farming town for some time, and the farmers are close to losing their entire crop of corn. It is the kind of situation, the film makes clear, that only the most hardened impostor like Jonas would take advantage of. His justification for his actions, when confronted by the town's sheriff, is that he puts on a good show and it will brighten people's spirits. It does not matter what you believe or even whether you believe at all, he claims, as long as you get the job done. For Jonas, of course, the job is twofold: to entertain and to rob. As events turn out, Jonas is undone by the handicapped brother of a waitress he is hoping to seduce.

The film is not afraid to suggest the possibility of the miracles that faith can effect. We are reminded of Jesus' instruction to the disciples of John the Baptist, all pointed images for the advent of the Kingdom of God: "Go and tell John what you hear and see: the blind recover their sight, the lame walk, the lepers are made clean, the deaf hear, the dead are raised to life, the poor are hearing the good news—and happy is the man who does not find me a stumbling-block" (Matthew 11:4-6). In the final scene, as abundant rain falls on the parched earth—almost despite Jonas's fake prayers—it seems evident that even Jonas wants to change. If his conversion is too much to hope for, he has at least abandoned his fraudulent ministry, and we are reminded that the Spirit transforms the soul as well as heals the body.

Holy Catholic Church:
Life-Giving Rituals

It was the Father's plan for our salvation that, in exalting his Son, he would send us the Spirit to carry on the Son's merciful work of transforming the world through love. The advent of the Holy Spirit at Pentecost, therefore, conferred upon the apostles and disciples of Jesus a mission and, through the community they created, that mission was passed on to Jesus' followers through the centuries. At Pentecost, stewardship becomes discipleship, and discipleship implies membership. The community of faith and mission that the creed calls "the holy catholic church" is for believers the ultimate visible sign of the presence of the Spirit in the world.

The union effected by the Holy Spirit is visible to all in "the holy catholic church," yet not limited historically or geographically to it. The gathering of believers that we call the *Church* is both holy and catholic. It is *holy* because it possess the life-giving rituals of salvation, and even though holiness can safely be applied to those who are becoming holy through faith in Christ and participation in the life of the sacraments, we are surely not claiming that all have achieved the perfection that is associated with sanctity. In fact, short of a rare gift of the Spirit, we understand that we are sinful members of the Church as long as our pilgrimage endures.

When we profess the Church as *catholic*, we mean that it exists for all peoples at all times and in all places. The mission of believers is precisely to gather everyone into the fold. Although this article of the Apostles' Creed in contrast to the next—"the communion of saints"—seems concerned with the visible Church, the term *Church* has from time to time been used erroneously against those who do not belong to the visible, historical community of the Church, as if to suggest that they are deprived of the means of salvation. We must recall, on the contrary, that the tradition of the Church has always been to acknowledge the membership of those who, although not actually baptized, either desire baptism or accept martyrdom for the faith. Although ours is not, by stated purpose, a context for theological debate or even for discussion of contemporary speculation about membership (as, for example, of Karl Rahner's liberating category of "anonymous Christians"), it is safe to say that even though this article celebrates the standard norm of membership in the Church— namely, visible membership—we have always and legitimately acknowledged membership that is not visible.

The visible Church is universally recognized by its sacramental rituals, and this is where fiction offers special nourishment. We have already had occasion, when discussing the efficacy of Jesus' redemptive death, to appeal to certain notable fictional reflections on the central role in our lives of the Eucharist, the primal sacrament of the Church. The other six sacraments, especially baptism, find their unifying significance in relation to the Eucharist, and to the extent that they are literally present in fiction, they give *explicit* testimony to our faith in the life-giving Spirit who sustains the Church; where there are literary or cinematic analogues to the sacraments—as is the case in most of the works I will appeal to—the testimony is *implicit*, but nonetheless effective.

In his novel *The Last Gentleman*, Walker Percy creates a fictional world, like ours, in which baptism is the principal event signaling our entrance into the Church—and the traditional sign of membership. By its climactic place in the action of the novel, baptism is also the surest sign that Will

Barrett, whose quest the novel traces, has taken his first tentative step toward a life of meaning. Like all of Percy's central characters, Barrett is looking for a sign. And it is surely no coincidence that, as with Jesus' "wicked, godless generation" (see Matthew 12:39), no sign is given to Barrett save the sign of the prophet Jonah—in this instance, baptism's ritual participation in the death and resurrection of Jesus.

The story begins in New York City and ends in New Mexico; in the language of Percy's narrative, it goes from "Ground Zero" to "the locus of pure possibility," or from the expectation of apocalypse to the realization of a new beginning. Barrett, using his telescope in Central Park, discovers in his line of magnified vision a woman sitting on a bench. That a telescope mediates reality to him tells us a lot about his distance from normal human relationships. In the course of events, following up on the drama that he watches from a safe distance unfolding before him, he meets the Vaughts, a family that he links his destiny to, when he discovers that the spot in the park where the woman had been sitting was precisely at "Ground Zero" of an imagined nuclear attack on New York City—and thus "a sign." The Vaughts are in New York seeking medical help for Jamie, their sixteen-year-old son, who has "a severe and atypical mononucleosis" that he is not expected to recover from, although he may have brief periods of remission. Barrett agrees to be his companion and eventually follows him to New Mexico, mainly because he has been commissioned by Jamie's sister Val, a Catholic nun, to be sure that he is baptized. It is a mission that Barrett feels thoroughly unequal too; he nonetheless *acts*, by summoning a priest to baptize Jamie, when it is clear that he is dying. This sacramental rite, in the design of the novel, is a sign of not only Jamie's salvation but also Barrett's because it signals his new life of personal meaning—"to make a contribution," as he puts it, "however small." *The Last Gentleman* is an odyssey of the Spirit, one of modern American literature's thoroughly life-affirming novels.

Flannery O'Connor's short story "A Temple of the Holy Ghost" underscores our sense of the grace of the sacrament of confirmation, even though there is no reference in the story to the sacrament as such and the only ritual explicitly appealed to is benediction of the blessed sacrament. This story is therefore a perfect example of our need as readers to delve beneath the literal level of the narrative to an analysis of the imagery and symbolism that share their meaning indirectly. In "A Temple of the Holy Ghost," those elements are obviously related to our traditional understanding of the sacrament that celebrates our special relationship to the Holy

Spirit at that awkward early adolescent time in our lives of maturing belief and developing commitment. The catechesis of the pre-Vatican II Church, which the story reflects, proclaimed the Spirit's desire to make us soldiers of Christ, even to the point of giving our lives for the faith.

The story centers around a weekend visit from a convent school by two teenage girls, Joanne and Susan, to the home of their second cousins, referred to simply as "the child" and "her mother." The girls are obsessed with boys and with their own appearance, and act obnoxiously as if they know everything. They parody Sr. Perpetua's instruction in defense of their purity, by referring to one another as "Temple One" and "Temple Two." What the nun had said, not surprisingly, was that if a young man were to "behave in an ungentlemanly manner with them in the back of an automobile," they were to protest by saying, "Stop sir! I am a Temple of the Holy Ghost!" The child's mother, convinced that she cannot entertain the girls all weekend, arranges dates to take them to a fair. As a result, the teenagers become the inadvertent instruments of spiritual growth for the child, who is, by her own admission, both "mean" and "sassy." Their report about the circus hermaphrodite becomes the occasion for the child's confirmation in the grace of self-acceptance.

At one point, the child, thinking about possible careers, daydreams about being a martyr, especially "if they killed her quick." In glamorous De Mille fashion, she rehearses her martyrdom, but each time she reaches the entrance into paradise, she returns to the lions that had cowered submissively in her presence, a foreshadowing of her final realization of her need for submission. The hermaphrodite's warning—"God made me thisaway and if you laugh He may strike you the same way"—returns to her dreamy imagination later on while she is gazing at the benediction host in the convent chapel, when she and her mother have taken the girls back to school. She recalls other words of the circus freak—"I don't dispute it; this is the way He wanted me to be"—and the association of host and hermaphrodite is a reminder that God himself, becoming man, accepted the limitations of the human condition and in becoming bread for remembrance reduced himself to the lowly form of everyday food. In the likeness of the hermaphrodite, the child comes to realize what her limitations are, but, more importantly, what she can accomplish despite them.

"Temple" in the title is singular precisely because the child is the one who genuinely struggles with the meaning of her special relationship with the Holy Spirit, but also to emphasize the universal implications of the story—namely, the dispositions each of us must have to be "a temple of the Holy Ghost." One of the reasons, no doubt, aside from the splendor of the production, that *The Wizard of Oz* is such a perennial classic is Dorothy's final realization that "there's no place like home" (in the minds of parents, good advice to children not to go wandering off). The film also supports the belief, implicit in "A Temple of the Holy Ghost," that the way we look upon others—and ourselves—makes all the difference in the world in our ability to treat them with the dignity they deserve.

Although the sacramental rituals of the visible Church seek the transformation of every aspect of our lives, there are, appropriately enough, special rites devoted to the preservation of the race through the creative love of marriage and to the continuation through ordination of an official, public ministry of sanctification within the community of belief. The emphasis on marriage and holy orders, which will be my focus here, is of course without prejudice in any way to the sanctification of the lives of committed single individuals, which of course is grounded in confirmation and strengthened regularly through the sacraments of reconciliation and the Eucharist. There have been some excellent films about the liberating ministry of orders, from the life of the priest to the ideal simplicity of the pope. Two films mentioned earlier in other contexts—*The Mission*, in part one, and *Mass Appeal*, in part two—will reward screening here too for obvious reasons, for their presentations respectively of missionary work on a grand scale and the "little way" of urban eucharistic ministry. Robert Young's *Saving Grace*, although not nearly as well known as *The Mission* and *Mass Appeal*, imagines a warmhearted Pope Leo XIV (not unlike the sort of pontiff Pope John Paul I seemed as if he would be), who accidentally locks himself out of a Vatican garden. Happy for the chance to be free for the moment from his cardinal overprotectors, he helps a mountain village survive extinction by uniting the people in an effort to rebuild their aqueduct. It is the power of love, not authority, that transforms a whole community; the combined imagery of pope, unity, water, and rebirth speaks for itself.

The very best stories of the Lifegiver reflecting the sacrament of matrimony have, to my mind, shown its dignity as the goal of a process of gradually unfolding friendship and love. Frank Capra's *It Happened One Night*, the first film ever to win all five major Academy Awards (best film, actor, actress, director, and writer), makes excellent viewing not only because it is one of the great romantic comedies of all times, but especially because of its treatment of marriage. Ellen Andrews, fleeing her father's yacht to rejoin the flyer she had eloped with, tries to travel incognito from Miami to New York by night bus. Her chance companion is Peter Warne, a reporter from New York, who recognizes her from newspaper photos, but declines to turn her over to the pursuing authorities her father has unleashed. The journey up the coast like all quests is fraught with set-backs; it takes four days, or rather four *nights*. The "it" of the title that happens "one night" is doubtlessly their realization, on the fourth night, that they have fallen in love. Twice during the trip, when they share accommodations at Warne's insistence (pretending that Ellen is married is her best protection), he suspends a blanket from a rope between their beds, calling it the "walls of Jericho." The innocence of the conceit is refreshing and reassuring, particularly at a time when falling in bed invariably pre-cedes falling in love, if the latter ever occurs. Falling in love is a process, unfolding in time and space, that has little if anything to do with what we have, and everything to do with who we are. Needless to say, in Capra's film the walls come tumbling down only when, further obstacles over-come, the two are married.

Since the 1930s and '40s, the period that produced the great romantic comedies like *It Happened One Night*, it is hard, especially after the demise of the production code in the late 1960s, to find films that present, however indirectly, an affirmative image of the love between man and woman that seems sympathetic to mainline Christian values related to marriage. *Bull Durham*, Ron Shelton's romantic comedy with a minor league baseball setting, comes close to the mark. Its love triangle has a rookie pitcher and the seasoned catcher brought in to train him vying, in vastly different ways, for the affections of a junior college English teacher and baseball enthusiast. Annie's devotion to baseball, and to baseball play-ers, seems to be a parody of religion; she even calls it her religion and keeps enough vigil lights in her house to rival a shrine. The back of her front door is a collage of evidence in support of her claim that she has prayed to "Buddha, Allah, Brahma, Vishnu, Shiva, trees, mushrooms, and Isadora Duncan." Since American film is still mostly shy about explicit appeals to religion (except perhaps, from the late '60s on, as a basis for satire), Annie's collage is as fine an indirect reference to the potentially sacred dimensions of the love latent in her affairs as we may hope to find.

Bull Durham's affirmation results from a contrast of relationships. Annie's fling with the pitcher Nuke, shown in a manner both literate and playful, nonetheless presents sex as a stage in a relationship to be built toward; yet theirs remains an arrangement of dependency. Not so with the friendship between Annie and the catcher, Crash. When they get together, it will be as equals. Crash seems to know it from the beginning; Annie has to learn it. And as they interact through the film's entire length, there's plenty of chemistry, but it is not an invitation to instant coupling. Their interaction, a mating game in the finest sense, is the source of the film's confident energy. Their physical intimacy is built so obviously on a developing personal union that it suggests the permanent commitment that faith associates with marriage.

In the subtle but accessible mode of comedy, *Bull Durham* suggests the mystical dimension of eros. The film's final shot, of Annie and Crash dancing, is an unforgettable image of the celebration of love as life's gracious gift, as affirmative and reassuring as any we are likely to find in contemporary cinema. Moreover, the film is rich in values that we all need to be reminded of from time to time—how exciting life can be when we know and confidently accept ourselves and our limitations, how rewarding work can be when we enjoy what we are doing and embrace it with enthusiasm, and how fulfilling love can be when we give it time to unfold, our very best time.

We have already had occasion, in part two, to appeal to the eucharistic imagery that is at the heart of Flannery O'Connor's *The Violent Bear It Away*—a hunger for the bread of life that only the banquet of the kingdom can fully satisfy. The novel plainly nurtures our faith in both baptism and Christian burial, the rites of entrance and departure that are central to the structure of O'Connor plot. In Mason's fundamentalist education of Tarwater, baptism and burial are the most important ritual acts in everyone's life. Insofar as Mason's desire to be given a proper Christian burial frames the novel, it seems appropriate to consider it here as a fictional variation on our belief that the sacraments sustain even our departure from life, converting the potential loneliness of dying and death into the certain expectation of resurrection.

Before Mason died, he had given his grandnephew Tarwater two specific commands: first, to provide him with a proper Christian burial, and then to go baptize his nephew Rayber's retarded son, Bishop (whom the agnostic Rayber had been successfully protecting from, what he considered, the old man's silly and meaningless rituals). These are the goals that drive the dramatic action of the novel, as well as the apparent incentives for Tarwater's final decision to accept the call to the prophetic life. As determined to reject Mason's mission as he is to rid himself of his hunger for the bread of life, Tarwater, in the beginning of the novel, burns down the house the old man dies in, thinking that he has taken the first step toward thwarting Mason's plans. Then he heads for the city, intending to complete his denial of Mason's requests. Mason's failure to baptize Bishop had proved to Tarwater that the old man was always saying "yes," but could not "*do* yes," and so in Tarwater's mind, Mason fell far short of the happiness Jesus promised "those who hear the word of God and keep it" (see Luke.11:28). As proof of his rejection of the call, Tarwater, intending to kill Bishop, wants to both "*say* no" and "*do* no." Ironically, though, just as he drowns his cousin, he blurts out the words of baptism. Although he will protest later, "The words just come out of themselves but it don't mean nothing," we know—and O'Connor certainly expects us to know— that the effectiveness of baptism does not depend upon the disposition or even the faith of the minister.

Thus, at the novel's conclusion, when Tarwater returns to the charred ruins of his home and discovers that Buford had buried Mason before Tarwater set fire to the house, the boy realizes that both of the old man's commands had in fact been obeyed. The novel is far more complex, of course, in its structure and motivation than this brief summary implies; nonetheless, the satisfaction of Mason's two wishes are unmistakable signs that Mason has created in Tarwater a true disciple. When he turns finally toward the city to "warn the children of God of the terrible speed of mercy," we know that Tarwater has accepted the call to a life of prophecy.

To end this section on fictional representations of the sacraments, I appeal again to Walker Percy's first novel, *The Moviegoer*, precisely because it provides us with a clear picture of the capacity of the sacra- ments to touch every aspect of our lives and thus to effect our sanctification. Although it is, first and foremost, the story of a young adult's confused search for some meaning in a life bordering on despair, Percy provides his narrator (Binx Bolling)—and us—with an unmistakable image of the ideal goal of such a quest: the near sanctity of Binx's half-brother, Lonnie Smith.

With masterful though subtle strokes, Percy celebrates the fullness of sacramental grace. Suffering from a terminal neurological disorder (pre- sumably cerebral palsy) and confined to a wheelchair, Lonnie shares with Binx both a love of movies and the secrets of his own spiritual conflicts. It is their discussions of the latter that give us a true glimpse of Lonnie's ascent to perfection, and by implication the effect of the Spirit's sanctifying power.

Midway in the week before Binx's thirtieth birthday (the period that the novel covers), Lonnie, almost fourteen, tells Binx that he is fasting in order "to conquer an habitual disposition." Binx protests on the grounds that Lonnie has already had pneumonia twice that year and is too weak to fast, but Lonnie says that his confessor is allowing it. When Binx asks what disposition, Lonnie admits that he still envies his older brother, Duval, who had drowned the previous summer. Apparently, they have discussed this before, but Binx does not understand how one can envy someone who is dead. With the insight of one struggling not with sins, but against imperfections, Lonnie explains, "Envy is not merely sorrow at another's good fortune: it is also joy at another's misfortune." Binx reminds Lonnie that he has already confessed his envy and received absolution, yet, as Binx narrates the encounter, Lonnie insists:

> "I'm still glad he's dead."
> "Why shouldn't you be? He sees God face to face and you don't."
> Lonnie grins at me with the liveliest sense of our complicity. . . . He knows that I have entered the argument as a game played by his rules and he knows that I know it, but he does not mind.
> "Jack, do you remember the time Duval went to the field meet in Jackson and won first in American history and the next day made all-state guard?"
> "Yes."
> "I hoped he would lose."
> "That's not hurting Duval."
> "It is hurting me. You know what capital sin does to the life of the soul."
> "Yes. Still and all I would not fast. Instead I would concentrate on the Eucharist. It seems a more positive thing to do."
> "That is true. . . . But Eucharist is a sacrament of the living."
> "You don't wish to live?"
> "Oh sure!" he says laughing, willing, wishing even, to lose the argument so that I will be sure to have as much fun as he.

Just before Binx leaves the Smiths' fishing camp, Lonnie tells his half-brother, knowing the depths of Binx's struggle against despair, "I am still offering my communion for you." It is another of Percy's special touches that Lonnie does not call his brother Binx, but rather Jack, the nickname for his given Christian name John [Bickerson Bolling].

By analogy to a flash-forward in film, anticipating the final article of the Apostles' Creed, it seems reasonable to note here how the novel's brief

Epilogue, which recounts the main events of the following year right up to the day before Lonnie dies, offers one of contemporary literature's most touching references to the resurrection of the flesh. Whereas the Epilogue suggests a tentative resolution to Binx's agonizing search for some meaning in his life (as we noted in part two), it leaves no doubt about Lonnie's achievement through the Spirit of the goal of Christian life—his experience of complete forgiveness at the time of his last anointing, the sacrament of the sick and dying. Binx and Kate, his cousin by marriage and now his wife, visit Lonnie in the hospital. It is Kate's first sight of Lonnie since the onset of his final illness, and she is unprepared for what she sees. Afterwards, outside of the hospital, Kate, "blind with tears," asks Binx what it was that Lonnie had whispered in his ear. "He told me that he had conquered an habitual disposition," Binx says, but ignores her request for an explanation by adding, "He also said you were a very good-looking girl." Binx seeks out his other half-brothers and sisters—all younger than Lonnie—who have been brought to the hospital by his mother, but left outside in the car. When he tells them that Lonnie is very sick, in fact dying, they are relieved to know that he has been anointed. Mathilde, aware of the special relationship between Lonnie and Binx, protests, "We love him, too!" Then, Donice, one of the twins, asks about the future with the simplicity that endeared children to Jesus:

> "Binx," [Donice] says . . . "When Our Lord raises us up on the last day, will Lonnie be in a wheelchair or will he be like us?"
> "He'll be like you."
> "You mean he'll be able to ski?" The children cock their heads and listen like old men.
> "Yes."
> "Hooray!" cry the twins. . . .

We can safely assume at this point in Binx's discovery of self that he is not simply telling the children what they want to hear, but confessing his own faith in the resurrection.

Communion of Saints:
Here and Hereafter

When we profess our belief in the *communion of saints*, we are not simply acknowledging our union with the blessed of the Kingdom of God: the *saints* are also our fellow pilgrims here on earth, both those who share the fellowship of the communion table as well as those who have, in fact, been confirmed in love by the Spirit even if they are not visible members of the universal Church. The earliest explanations of the creed suggested that "communion of saints" was first and foremost a confession of belief in the life-giving power of the Eucharist inasmuch as the Latin word translated as "saints"—*sanctorum*—also means "the holy objects," that is to say, the bread and wine that become for us the body and blood of Christ. Since the Eucharist is our principal ritual of sanctification, it is the celebration and remembrance that begins, sustains, and hopefully will complete the Spirit's process of making us holy. It is also, necessarily, the norm of self-sacrifice by which the Spirit confirms in grace those even who have never shared in the communion table—the hidden saints the world over.

Once again we have occasion to appeal to *The Grapes of Wrath*, this last time as nourishing our faith in the life-giving Spirit. When Tom Joad bids farewell to his mother, his sense of mission following Jim Casy's self-sacrifice has the ring of a believer's appropriate response to Jesus' instruction, "Do this in remembrance of me." "You know what I been thinking about—'bout Casy," Tom tells his mother, "'bout what he said, what he done, 'bout how he died, and I remember all of it." Then, Tom tries to comfort his mother about not knowing where he will be or what he will be doing, as he follows Casy's inspiration:

> I'll be everywhere, wherever you can look. Wherever there's a fight so hungry people can eat, I'll be there. Wherever there's a cop beating up a guy, I'll be there. I'll be in the way guys yell when they're mad. I'll be in the way kids laugh when they're hungry and they know supper's ready. I'll be there. And when the people are eating the stuff they raise and living in the houses they build, I'll be there too.

Tom's effort to console his mother is clearly a variation on the theme of the communion of saints.

In treating fictional analogues to Jesus' resurrection, we have already considered Terry Malloy's growth in *On the Waterfront* from the level of a manipulated prizefighter to become a champion of workers' rights. The character in the film who is perhaps most instrumental in directing Terry's conversion is Fr. Barry, modeled on Fr. Corridan's heroic life as "the waterfront priest." After an informer is brutally murdered in the hold of a ship, Fr. Barry urges the men not to be intimidated by such criminal tactics by the mob-controlled leadership of the longshoremen's union. His powerful sermon is an application of our belief in the Church as the mystical body of Christ, a vision of unity comparable to the communion of saints. It is Christ, he insists, who has just died again in slain longshoreman. In the direct language of a man of action, he shouts: "Boys, this is my Church. And if you don't think Christ is down here on the waterfront, you got another guess coming!" Karl Malden's portrayal of Fr. Barry is perhaps his finest performance, and one for which he won a richly deserved Oscar for best supporting actor.

There is, however, no more explicit representation in film of the communion of saints than the closing scene of Robert Benton's *Places in the Heart*. Only film as art has the capacity to achieve this sort of transcendent meaning. The literary text could not support it, nor could painting or one of the other static visual arts. Although these comments may seem overly theoretical at this point, they relate directly to my earlier observation about fiction's capacity to reach the whole person—psychologically, emotionally, intellectually, spiritually. I am referring, of course, to film's capacity to show us its meaning *in motion*. The visual surprise created by the camera's subtle shifts in movement supports Benton's final statement.

It is a scene though, as in all great films, that cannot stand on its own. Its meaning derives from its relationship to the whole story and its setting, but especially from its stark contrast to the story's tragic beginning. Even before the opening sequence, one has the sense from the visuals behind the credits that this town—Waxahachie, Texas—is a peaceful community despite its racial separation and even division. The year is 1935, the heart of the Great Depression. As the story begins, the Spaldings are seated at the dinner table, and Royce, father of the family and sheriff of Waxahachie, is giving thanks for their blessings. Two gunshots are heard in the distance at intervals during the blessing. Royce Spalding is abruptly called from the table by his deputies to subdue Wylie, a drunken black youth, whose escapades are apparently a regular occurrence in the town. Spalding tries to coax Wylie into giving himself up; Wylie fires his pistol into the air and, in a drunken spin, fires a final shot that hits and kills Royce. It is clearly one of those tragic accidents that we have come to know will happen, totally unexpected and completely unintended, but that nonetheless reshape the course of our lives. While Royce is being waked, the townsmen, almost as if by accepted ritual, drag Wylie through the streets and lynch him. Both men are buried the same morning, although in separate cemeteries.

The rest of the film, short of the final sequence, deals with Edna Spalding's efforts to support two children and save her house from foreclosure. Her sister, Margaret, scarcely making ends meet in her hairdressing shop, is unable to give Edna a job. So, with the advice and help of Moze, a homeless black drifter, she decides to plant cotton. The bank manager, bringing his blind cousin, Mr. Will, to live with her, insists that her only hope is to take in lodgers. We learn, too, that Margaret's husband, Wayne, is having an affair with the local schoolteacher. Through hard work that finally involves Edna's whole family and some black migrant workers, the cotton is picked in time to be sold at a price high enough to pay the amount due on her mortgage.

Their goal achieved, Moze decides to move on because he knows that the local Klansmen, furious about his bringing in the migrant workers, will not give up till they have punished him sufficiently; Mr. Will had foiled their first attempt, by recognizing their voices and disclosing their identities. Although their labor in the field is not over dramatized, it is presented with sufficient poetic realism—blazing suns and cut fingers and scratched hands against the pure white of the cotton—to give us a strong sense of the interpersonal dignity of human work that sustains as well as satisfies. In this regard, *Places in the Heart* is an ideal complement to *The Grapes of Wrath*, both films extolling the worker in the spirit of the papal encyclicals, the latter showing the determined quest for suitable work, the former the achievement of that goal.

Without the final scene, though, *Places in the Heart* would be less of an artistic achievement and have far less of a religious impact. We hear music from the local church before we see a long shot of the sparse congregation. As the minister introduces his text—the hymn to love from First Corinthians—we can easily identify Wayne and Margaret, sitting in the first row, reconciled, and behind them Mr. Will, Edna and her children, and the bank manager. When the choir rises to sing "In the Garden" and the minister pronounces the memorial words of the Last Supper, the communion plates—bread first, then wine—are passed through the congregation. The camera position shifts to a medium close shot, taking in two or three people at a time, and pans with the communion plates along the pews. This is the specific cinematic technique that supports this film's final commentary on community and illustrates film's capacity to transcend realism.

As the camera pans slowly along and new faces come into view, we notice gradually that the pews are now full and that everyone is present— the living and the dead, the present and the departed, the good and the bad, not just those faithful few who were scattered around the congregation at our first viewing of it. The Klansmen are there, without their robes of course, and so is Moze. But most astonishing of all, we see Royce standing next to Edna, and next to him Wylie. As if to end his film where it had begun, Benton shows Royce and Wylie together in the last frame, victim and unwilling murderer. Wylie receives communion from Royce and, looking back at him, smiles and says, "Peace of God." Whether or not it was Benton's intention to suggest the communion of saints, he has effectively reminded us that the whole Church—wayfaring, suffering and triumphant—is united at the eucharistic banquet.

Finally, there are two films about conflicting American lifestyles, worth noting here briefly and definitely worth viewing, that offer positive and negative images of the communion of saints. In Peter Weir's *Witness*, an Amish boy is the sole witness of a violent crime in Philadelphia. The detective protecting the boy—and himself—from corrupt city officials seeks refuge in the tranquil countryside and falls in love with an Amish woman. Before the action reaches a climax and the lovers realize their irreconcilable differences, the portrait of the Amish community—its sense of simplicity and harmony—gives clear witness, on a deeper level, to our understanding of the communion of saints. Arthur Penn's *Alice's Restaurant* contrasts the hippie drug subculture opposed to the Vietnam War with (exaggerated) mainstream American attitudes and values. Folk singer Arlo Guthrie, playing himself, takes to the road, after avoiding the draft, in a classic search for meaning that leads to the famous Trinity Church commune of Alice and Ray Brock near Stockbridge, Massachusetts. Repentance and forgiveness are at the heart of this portrait of a failed "communion of saints." *Alice's Restaurant* delivers a powerful feeling for a world gripped by the "eschatological" tensions of this phase of salvation history, reflected in some of the great American literary metaphors for the human experience—from Hawthorne's "troubled joy" ("The Maypole of Merry Mount") to Faulkner's "victorious dust" (*Absalom! Absalom!*).

Forgiveness of Sins:
Personal Transformation

Conversion, the change of heart necessary to embrace the Kingdom of God, implies that we have sought, and therefore believe in, the possibility of the forgiveness of our sins. Mark's Gospel begins with this announcement: "And so it was that John the Baptist appeared in the wilderness proclaiming a baptism in token of repentance, for the forgiveness of sins" (Mark 1:4). The grace to acknowledge our own sinfulness, though, makes a bloody entrance into our prideful hearts, as we noted at the beginning of this chapter in O'Connor's story of Asbury, "The Enduring Chill." Sacred Scripture's first and greatest story of all—the fall of our biblical first parents—reminds us constantly of the innate tendency of sinful humanity to point the finger at someone else. It is a baleful legacy of the history of sin that we call original sin.

When St. Luke in the Acts of the Apostles chose the image of "tongues" to describe the descent of the Holy Spirit on the apostles, he seemed consciously to have chosen, or so the Fathers of the Church believed, an image that would show the event of the Spirit at Pentecost as reversing the dire effects of the division of tongues at the tower of Babel: the metaphor of the Book of Genesis for the universality of sin as presumption. This is perhaps one of the clearest instances in the Bible of the power of the poetic image to capture realities that transcend the reach of everyday language. The following brief, but classic passage from a sermon on Pentecost by St. Fulgentius of Ruspe demonstrates the antiquity of the Church's acceptance of the place of metaphor in elaborating our understanding of our faith:

> For just as after the flood the wicked pride of men built a high tower against the Lord, and the human race then deserved to be divided by means of a diversity of languages so that each people speaking its own tongue was no longer understood of the others; so the humble piety of the faithful has made these diverse tongues combine in the unity of the church, so that what discord had broken up love should reunite, and the scattered members of humanity, as members of one only body, should be bound up together in Christ, the only head, and forged together in the fire of love to make the unity of this holy body.

If the punishment for sin and its spread throughout the world is presented in terms of our inability to understand the language of others (see Genesis 11:7), then surely we are to believe that the effects of sin have been radically reversed when, with the gift of the Spirit, people hear a foreign language as if it were their own being spoken (see Acts 2:6). Thus, in professing our faith in "the forgiveness of sins," we acknowledge the unifying action of the Holy Spirit as the Person who, sent by the Father in the name of Jesus, effects the forgiveness of our sins and thus builds up the body of love—the Church—whose head is Christ.

In this context, we must remember that Jesus himself told the first and greatest story ever of the Lifegiver—the parable of the prodigal son—as recorded in St. Luke's Gospel (see 15:11–32). In fact, a major theme of Luke's Gospel is forgiveness. His fifteenth chapter introduces the well-known parable by comparing the heavenly joy over the repentance of a sinner to the everyday experiences of finding a lost sheep and a lost coin. When Jesus explains his first comparison by asserting that "there will be greater joy in heaven over one sinner who repents than over ninety-nine righteous people who do not need to repent," he is not, however, preparing his listeners to distinguish between the two sons in the parable he is about to tell. Although we may be inclined to look upon the repentance and forgiveness of the younger son as exhausting the meaning of the parable, we should note carefully that the story actually provides us with examples of two types of sinfulness: the younger son, who leaves his father's house and degrades himself beyond imagining, and the older son, who remains with the father but without understanding or compassion.

The younger son not only lives recklessly but also seems to abandon his faith when, starving in that "distant country," he goes to work for a gentile landowner, feeding hogs (animals considered unclean by the Jews), but is denied even a morsel of their food. Repenting, he returns to his father and asks only to be treated as one of his paid servants, his expectations suggesting the humility that repentance requires. His father's response, however, indicates clearly the undeserved bounty of the grace of forgiveness. The older son, on the other hand, when a feast is prepared for his brother, resents his father's mercy and envies his brother's good fortune. He typifies those of us whose service in our Father's house is grudging and whose disposition is self-righteous. Repentance, the parable makes quite clear, precedes forgiveness. The older son, whose sinfulness by all counts is lesser than his brother's, does not apparently repent and so is not forgiven. The story ends abruptly with the father's tender admonition of his elder son: "My boy, . . . you are always with me, and everything I have is yours. How could we help celebrating this happy day? Your brother here was dead and has come back to life, was lost and is found."

As I have tried to show in *Image and Likeness*—a collection of essays on the Jewish-Christian dimensions of American film classics—*The Godfather* films are a cinematic trilogy that rivals the very best of American fiction. The first two films can be viewed in the context of "the forgiveness of sins" as indictments of the hypocritical or hardened heart, which is a central religious symbol of the American Puritan literary tradition. It is

The Godfather Part III, though, that deals explicitly with the agonies of redemption, with the saving grace of forgiveness itself as it labors to transform the troubled human heart.

The middle-aged Don Michael Corleone, seeming sincere in his desire to turn away from a life of crime, seeks a reconciliation with his children—and with his Church. All Corleone business interests, he insists, have gone legitimate. A major contributor to Vatican charities, Michael tries through his lawyer to assume control of Vatican investments in return for his help in liquidating Vatican debts. Frustrated in his efforts with both family and Church, he takes on finally the tragic dimensions of Shakespeare's King Lear. How this all works out under the masterful direction of Francis Coppola needs to be viewed, of course, in its intricate and spellbinding detail. The heart of the film as story of the Lifegiver, though, occurs when the Don, fearing that the same criminal elements he battled in the United States have penetrated the chambers of Vatican finance, visits Cardinal Lamberto because he has been described as someone Michael can really trust. (Shortly thereafter, Lamberto becomes pope, but with a brief reign reminiscent of John Paul I's.) The cardinal takes a stone from a fountain, breaks it in half to show its dry inside, illustrating for Michael how slow the human heart is to accept forgiveness.

> *Lamberto:* See this stone. It's been in the water, and the water hasn't penetrated it. The same thing has happened to men in Europe. They've been surrounded by Christianity for centuries, but Christ hasn't penetrated their hearts. Would you like to confess?
> *Michael:* I'm beyond redemption. What use is it to confess if I don't repent. I betrayed my wife, my self, had my brother killed, my mother's son, my father's son.
> *Lamberto:* It is just that you have suffered much. Your life can be redeemed, but I know you don't believe that.

The cardinal is saintly enough to draw from Michael his deepest secrets, an acknowledgment of his most heinous sin—conspiring to have his own brother killed. Although the cardinal knows that there has been a kind of retributive justice to his suffering, he is also aware that Michael is close to committing a sin against the Holy Spirit, in feeling that he is beyond redemption. It is in this sense that Coppola's film is about the very possibility of our experiencing God's merciful forgiveness. Only when we accept forgiveness can we begin to live for the reunification of the human family.

Tim Robbins's *Dead Man Walking* is perhaps a more focused example of the absolute necessity for "forgiveness" if there is to be a community of belief. Sister Helen Prejean, as the fictional version of her real-life story goes, is living and working in a black project in New Orleans when, in response to a talk she has given on capital punishment, a death row inmate at Angola, the state's maximum security prison, asks her to come visit him. Despite the fact that she finds Matthew Poncelet's attitude reprehensible, she agrees to be his spiritual advisor. Her task, against all apparent odds, is to get Poncelet to admit his crime, in effect to take responsibility for his actions. Poncelet, however, insists on his own innocence, that he was just a bystander, claiming that his companion, acquitted because his family could afford a high-powered defense team, was the one who raped and murdered Hope Percy and then shot her boyfriend, Walter Delacroix. At one point, Sr. Helen asks Poncelet if he ever reads the Bible, quoting John's Gospel for him—and the verse becomes the heart of her ministry—"If you dwell within the revelation I have brought, . . . you shall know the truth, and the truth will set you free" (Jesus in the Temple, speaking to the Jews who believed in him; John 8:32).

As Poncelet slowly moves toward an acknowledgment of the truth, Sr. Helen grows gradually and painfully into an acceptance of her calling to this prison ministry, and into a fuller sense of her own inner strength as she deals with the scorn of the parents of the dead youths, the condescension of the prison chaplain, her own mother's anxiety, and even her temporary rejection by the blacks in the project who cannot understand why she is trying to help a white racist criminal. The critic Gene Siskel expressed it succinctly when he wrote that "*Dead Man Walking* is really about the capacity of this nun's heart to absorb the evil, pain and suffering of those around her and still embrace the sanctity of a human life." Sister Helen and Matthew Poncelet both achieve higher levels of self-realization as a result of their laborious dialogue; and as they grow together in mutual acceptance and understanding, composition of frame confirms their growth visually—from shot-reverse-shot, through medium two-shots, to actual physical contact when Sr. Helen is allowed to place her hand on his shoulder as he marches to his execution. In his final moments, Poncelet tells Sr. Helen: "I didn't think I'd have to die to find love. Thanks for loving me." For him, she sings, however falteringly, the hymn "Be Not Afraid." And at the end, she invites him to look at her, saying simply, "I want you to see the face of love." This film, which at its center is a film against killing, no matter who does it, criminal or the state, is also on a much deeper level about growth toward genuine personhood through the labor of love and forgiveness.

This is an appropriate place for us to complete our examination of Lawrence Kasdan's film *Grand Canyon*, that was introduced as a story of the Creator. There are many ways in which this film, if it is allowed to work its miracle in our hearts, can nourish our faith, but one of the most obvious is the way in which it treats the possibility of "miracles" themselves—those grace-filled, Spirit-charged experiences, completely out of the ordinary, that unexpectedly dissolve our sinful differences and unite us to one another. Mack, we have already noted, is saved from almost certain death because he is a white man in the inner city at night—the wrong place at the wrong time. His savior is Simon, a black man who lives and works in the inner city. The following morning, while Mack's wife, Claire, is jogging through their affluent neighborhood, she hears an infant cry and, searching through the brush in a woodsy area, discovers an abandoned baby girl. Claire is convinced that there is a reason she found her. It is like Simon's being in the right place at the right time to save Mack, she argues. "Some kind of connection has been made and it has to be played out," she insists. And then she raises the possibility of a miracle. "What if these are miracles, Mack?" she asks. "Maybe we don't have any experience with miracles so we're slow to recognize them." Mack claims to have a "terrific headache," but Claire refuses to believe it, insisting, "It is an inappropriate response to get a headache in the presence of a miracle."

Although this sort of exchange is typical of the film's humor and its effort to soften the religious references, there is no doubt that the Kasdans want us to believe that we have witnessed two miracles. There is further evidence in the film that events happen that can only be explained by postulating a purposeful universe, and that is the reason why the film also nourishes our belief in God the Creator. Mack recalls for Simon another time in his life when he was saved from death by a woman, who pulled him back from in front of a fast-moving bus on Los Angeles's Miracle Mile (the choice of place was surely no coincidence). All he had a chance to do at the time was thank the woman, who responded, "My pleasure!" Her wearing a Pirates cap was another bond between them because Pittsburgh is his favorite baseball team. One of the reasons Mack refuses to let Simon out of his life is due to his regret that he had no further contact with his earlier savior. And, on another day, while Claire is jogging, a homeless man, whom she has been frightened by before, clearly tells her as she runs by, "Keep the baby. You need her as much as she needs you."

Because the "miracles" of the film serve to bring people together, to create new bonds of love and friendship, *Grand Canyon* is also a story of the Lifegiver. It is the Spirit who "makes connections"—to use the language of the script. Connecting people who are otherwise divided by the barriers of contemporary society is an obvious illustration of the powerful image used by Luke and Fulgentius that we saw earlier—with the advent of the Spirit, tongues no longer divide, but unite.

Inasmuch as the Spirit's impulse toward conversion inspires us at the least to rise above our lower inclinations, John Huston's film *The African Queen*, set in German East Africa at the beginning of World War I, makes a satisfying story of the Lifegiver. It traces a journey with a mission down one of Africa's more treacherous waterways from a Methodist Missionary compound to a lake at the river's mouth. Humphrey Bogart and Katharine Hepburn play the principal characters with charm and conviction. Charlie Allnut, the Canadian captain of the riverboat *African Queen*, is zany enough until he comes under the guidance of the British spinster missionary Rosie Sayer, who says all the right things. The mission—to destroy the German warship *Louisa*—is Rosie's patriotic idea, no doubt in partial retribution for the Germans' destroying the Mission compound and for causing the tragic death of her brother. The film, whose central image for the quest for self-transcendence is the river itself, exudes a feeling, too, for a purposeful universe, the confidence that comes from trust in a benevolent deity, and as such nourishes our faith in God the Creator. Things do not always work out as planned by the film's central figures, far from it; but when they do, Charlie and especially Rosie seem aware of their partnership in a providential plan.

The *African Queen* is also, and perhaps more pointedly, about our need to aim high, to transcend the pull of our lower inclinations, and for this reason we consider it here as a story of the Lifegiver. No doubt the film's best line is Rosie's response to Charlie's feeble defense of his occasional excesses in drinking, claiming that it is only human nature. Rosie retorts, "Nature, Mr. Allnut, is what we have been put in this world to rise above."

Finally, two strongly recommended films that demonstrate the personal transformation we believe is the effect of grace are John Ford's *The Searchers* and Bruce Beresford's *Tender Mercies*. In Ford's great western, Ethan Edwards, an exconfederate soldier who pursues the Comanche captors of his niece, is a man obsessed with prejudice against anyone tainted with Indian blood. When he discovers after an almost endless trek across the plains that the Comanche chief has taken the girl as his wife, we know that he will want to kill her. *The Searchers* is a perfect instance in fiction of how what one discovers at the end of a search is often vastly different from what one was looking for—namely, for Ethan, an opportunity to shed his prejudices in order to become more fully human.

Tender Mercies is a quietly effective story of the Lifegiver that contrasts the glitter and superficiality of the world of country music with the everyday values of work, family, and simple human kindness. An alcoholic singer finds rehabilitation through the care and concern of a widow and the genuine devotion of her son; these are life's tender mercies—and obvious gifts of the Spirit.

Resurrection of the Body: Hope Confirmed

True inner peace is born of our trust that we, too, will rise in glory with Jesus and share the unending life of God's kingdom. These are aspects of our faith that we know the least about when it comes to specific details. One thing, though, is perfectly clear: we believe that the whole person, body and soul, will be transformed and that it is not just the soul, separated from the body, that is to be immortal. Although the manner of this transformation is a mystery, the New Testament, especially in the letters of St. Paul, provides suggestions, couched as always in poetic language. In 1 Corinthians 15:35–38, Paul uses a harvest analogy; namely, that the risen body is to the earthly body as the full flower is to the seed. We also confidently hope—with Teilhard de Chardin, as we read in the Epigraph to part one—that the material things we accomplish or cherish will not perish either even if the mode of their transformation and presence is not known. Since as human beings we necessarily relate to others and to creation through our bodies and since our greatest joys, even our most penetrating insights, begin in the flesh, that is to say, in our senses, it is difficult to imagine a resurrection apart from the flesh.

Daniel Petrie's film *Resurrection* seems at first to be more about the "experience of dying" than it is about the subject of its title; nonetheless, as a powerful story of healing and love, it is in the final analysis very much about its title because it clearly portrays those gifts of the Spirit—healing and love—as witnesses to the Resurrection. This excellent film has had far too little exposure, but like all of the films discussed in this book, it is available at most video outlets. In the film's opening sequence, Edna McCauley dies in a tragic automobile accident with her husband, Joe, when he swerves to avoid hitting a little boy and their car goes over a cliff. After a brief experience of the marvels of the afterlife, she alone miraculously revives, although without any sensation in her lower legs. On the way home to Kansas in the care of her father, the kindly old proprietor of the Last Chance Gas station before the California desert shows Edna his prize two-headed snake, calling it one of God's miracles. A sign on the station wall quietly, but clearly declares, "God is love." Once home, Edna becomes aware of the fact that she has brought back from death the power to heal. She directs the energy in her hands against her own legs and feet, and soon she is able to walk without crutches. By this point in the film, Petrie has carefully led us to associate with God and resurrection the miraculous healing of flesh and spirit.

Raised to believe, but by a stern and unloving father, Edna herself seems to have lost her faith, but not her capacity to care for others, and even though she lives amid firm believers of every stripe, she is unwilling to name any source for her power other than love and the extraordinary experience she has had of the afterlife. The man she develops an intimate relationship with, Cal, although the renegade son of a fire-and-brimstone preacher, soon becomes obsessed by her ability to heal, and surprisingly demands that she "name the Holy Ghost" as the source of her evident gift. She is too modest, however, to go beyond the convictions that she has, so she protests to Cal, "If there's anything holy in what I do, it's the holiness of love." When Cal's fixation on her confessing her faith as she heals turns to near tragedy, Edna tells her grandmother, "Joan of Arc was burned for hearing voices, and I almost was for not hearing them." In the film's final scene, Edna (years later), as the sole proprietor of the Last Chance Gas Station, embraces with healing love a brave young boy with cancer—a gift that we are confident will be effective. It is clear to us then, if not before, that healing is the film's metaphor for sharing the talents we have bountifully and undeservedly received. The symbolism and the tone of the film leave us with little doubt that Edna's life-giving power is, indeed, the work of the Holy Spirit. Ellen Burstyn's performance as Edna is simply flawless and thus perfectly believable, and the special effects in light and sound of her entry into the life beyond death are both stunningly beautiful and profoundly moving.

For a fictional representation of the quest for solid grounds for our hope in the resurrection, we need look no further than John Updike's short story masterpiece "Pigeon Feathers." It is subtly, implicitly, a powerful story of the Lifegiver. In it an adolescent boy has to cope with the specter of death and the darkness of doubt before he experiences the epiphany that grounds his faith in life everlasting. Fourteen-year-old David Kern has just moved with his parents and grandmother from Olinger back to the farm that his grandparents had once owned. As he arranges some books on a shelf in a reluctant effort to help with the move, he "slips into" reading H. G. Wells's account of Jesus in *The Outline of History*. Stunned by the author's "fantastic falsehoods," he is horrified to think that, "at a definite spot in time and space a brain black with the denial of Christ's divinity has been suffered to exist." At dinner that evening, his parents continue their "endless argument about organic farming," his mother insisting that "the land has a *soul*," and if left alone the soil will rejuvenate itself. David's father, a chemistry major in college, insists that only chemical fertilizers can replace the chemicals in soil depleted in growing crops, adding emphatically, "Only human indi-vidu-als have souls." The reference to the human soul is no doubt momentarily comforting to David after his earlier encounter with Wells' virulent disbelief.

Later that evening, in the farm's outhouse, an insect alights on the flashlight that David has placed beside him, as a protection against spiders, and when he sees the insect's X-ray projected onto the wall, he is visited without warning "by an exact vision of death." Reluctant at first to expose his anxiety to his parents, but unable to rid himself of thoughts of extinction, he seeks and finds some solace in the concluding words of the unabridged Webster's Dictionary's definition of *soul*: "usually held to be separable [from the body] in existence." Then in catechetical class at the local Lutheran church, where—appropriately enough for our present context—the subject matter is "the last third of the Apostles' Creed," he puts his question to the Rev. Dobson: "About the Resurrection of the Body—are we conscious between the time when we die and the Day of Judgment?" When Dobson tells him that he supposes "not," and then adds insult to injury, as far as David is concerned, by suggesting that he should look upon heaven "as the way the goodness Abraham Lincoln did lives after him," David is outraged at the impudence of the minister's answers and, especially, his cowardice in refusing to say in a conversational voice what he professed every Sunday morning in the creed. Later, David gets equally evasive, if not negative, answers from his parents, although his mother finally says, "Honestly, David, I'm sure there will be something for us." Convinced that he is surrounded by some adult conspiracy of disbelief and fearing that "nowhere in the world of other people would he find the hint, the nod, he needed to begin to build his fortress against death," he nonetheless strives to keep "alive the possibility of hope" by looking for signs that even "somewhere, at sometime, someone had recognized that we cannot, *cannot*, submit to death."

Time passes, and for his fifteenth birthday, David's parents give him a Remington .22, "with jokes about him being a hillbilly now." Throughout the school year he happily puts off till the last minute the need to drive with his father back down the country road "into the heart of the dark farmland, where the only light [is] the kerosene lamp waiting on the dining-room table, a light that drown[s] their food in shadow and [makes] it sinister"—and that apparently too easily reminds David of death. During the summer, when his grandmother wants him to kill the pigeons that are fouling the furniture stored in the barn, he undertakes the task, reluctantly claiming that he is not particularly interested in killing anything. Nonetheless, while going against his inclination, he is rewarded with the most extraordinary revelation. Preparing to bury the six pigeons he has killed, he discovers the incredible beauty and intricate design of the birds' feathers: "Across the surface of the infinitely adjusted yet somehow effortless mechanics of the feathers played idle designs of color, no two alike, designs executed, it seemed, in a controlled rapture, with a joy that hung level in the air above and behind him." And as he places the last two pigeons in the ground, he receives the confirmation of his hope that he has so fervently sought:

> Crusty coverings were lifted from him, and with a feminine, slipping sensation along his nerves that seemed to give the air hands, he was robed in this certainty: that the God who had lavished such craft upon these worthless birds would not destroy His whole Creation by refusing to let David live forever.

In the least expected place and, no doubt, in part because he persisted with open mind in seeking confirmation of his belief, David is rewarded with the kind of certainty about the resurrection and life everlasting that he so obviously hoped for. If I have quoted at length from the story, it is because there is, I think, no one writing fiction today in America who uses words with greater precision and grace than John Updike.

Two decades ago, I wrote that Flannery O'Connor's short story "Judgement Day" is "perhaps our noblest literary presentation of the significance of resurrection." I am inclined now much less to consider my praise over-blown than to drop the *perhaps*. It is about an exile's return to his homeland and as such it evokes the triumphant homecoming that we anticipate the resurrection to be; that a story with this power would be the last one that O'Connor submitted for publication before her untimely death is one of the gentler ironies of literary history. Like most of O'Connor's truly great stories, "Judgement Day" dramatizes a convergence of human tensions on a variety of levels—between generations, races, classes, cultures, and worldviews.

Imprisoned in his daughter's New York apartment, Tanner wants to return to Corinth, Georgia, at any cost, "dead or alive"; he is willing to pay the price because he has come in his final days to admit his mistake in originally consenting to leave home. Apparently unaware that he has already had a minor stroke, he stubbornly plans his escape to the freedom of the southern countryside from the high-rise "pigeon-hutch of a build-ing." His anticipation of success erupts into a dream, the device that O'Connor uses so successfully to evoke the story's sense of ultimate vic-tory. Tanner's dream is pure wish-fulfillment; in it he arranges to escape from New York in a pine box so that he can play a joke on his backwoods cronies. When he gets to Corinth—alive in his dream, of course—he pops out of the coffin and shouts with great glee, scaring his friends half to death, "Judgement Day! Judgement Day! . . . Don't you two fools know it's Judgement Day!" Awakening from his dream, and with instructions about his destination pinned inside his coat, he totters into the hallway, lurches toward the stairs, and falls down half a flight. The jolt of his fall becomes in his imagination the unrelieved joy of a coffin sliding off the baggage wagon in Corinth.

What little help he actually gets comes in the form of a surly black actor who lives in the same apartment building. Their climactic and tragic encounter—that is ironically both judgment day and homecoming for Tanner—seems to be the unavoidable consequence of his actual sins of dishonesty to self, which led to his banishment, and his original sin of denial of human brotherhood, which accounts for his persistent lapses into racial condescension. If the story, like all of O'Connor's, is designed to show us the earthly consequences of our follies, it also suggests that Tanner, liberated from the purgatory of his exile, experiences a merciful resurrection when his daughter relents finally and ships his body home to Corinth for burial.

Life Everlasting:
Reflections of Fundamental Hope

The final phrase of the creed proclaims our faith in the glorious new creation that is to signal the end of time just as the first creation announced time's beginning. For the clearest explanation of the meaning for our lives today of our belief in "life everlasting," we turn to what is considered by many the greatest document of the Second Vatican Council, *Gaudium et Spes*, the Pastoral Constitution on the Church in the Modern World:

> While we are warned that it profits a man nothing if he gain the whole world and lose himself, the expectation of a new earth must not weaken but rather stimulate our concern for cultivating this one. For here grows the body of a new human family, a body which even now is able to give some kind of foreshadowing of the new age. Earthly progress must be carefully distinguished from the growth of Christ's Kingdom. Nevertheless, to the extent that the former can contribute to the better ordering of human society, it is of vital concern to the kingdom of God (Abbott, n. 39).

In Teilhard de Chardin's vision of our universe evolving toward the Omega Point, his image for the biblical fullness of time, we have, for all practical purposes, a fresh variation on traditional theology's association of heaven with the experience of divinization (God became human so that we might become divine) or of the beatific vision. The goal of evolution in a universe shaped by the Incarnation, Teilhard proposes, is our assimilation into the perfection of community that is the Holy Trinity. The Risen Christ draws us toward himself till that point when we have achieved, through the power of his Resurrection, perfect individuality *and* perfect community. We shall be *both* fully ourselves *and* totally united with others.

From the point of view of the impact of belief on our spiritual lives, no contemporary insight into the fulfillment of everlasting life has affected me more than the passage from C. S. Lewis's *The Great Divorce* that heads this chapter. When he says that the substance of what we often seek "even in [our] most depraved wishes will be there, beyond expectation," he is providing us with one of the powerful personal reasons for avoiding sin. For who can deny having "depraved wishes"? Moreover, who can deny the intense absorption of our attention by the happy times that we experience in our lives and the feeling afterwards that we had lost complete track of time? Eternity is, of course, the absence of time. Losing track of time can be a foretaste of life everlasting.

When it comes to stories that nourish our belief in life everlasting, it is perhaps ironic that science fiction, which many consider one of the lesser forms of fiction, often provides us, in its images of more perfect societies, with suggestions of the perfection of the kingdom and thus stimulates our sense of hope. Steven Spielberg's second and final cut of his film *Close Encounters of the Third Kind*, called *The Special Edition*, ends with an elaborate scene that allows the viewer to enter the spaceship with those who were called aboard. If the spaceship itself from the outside seems like a magnificent ornament for a galactic tree, its tiers of joyous spectators on the inside clearly suggest the many mansions that Jesus said are in his Father's house or, perhaps, the third heaven of St. Paul's ecstasy (see 2 Corinthians 12:2). The spectacular visuals are the perfect complement to the symphony of bells that announce the ship's ascent.

To the extent that our hope as Christians has a determined object, it is most surely in the resurrection of the body and the eternal life of the kingdom. Almost without exception, though, stories in both literature and film relate to the kind of hope that Gabriel Marcel has called fundamental hope or a hope apparently without a specific object or desire, as when we say simply "we hope" rather than "we hope that . . ." Some have suggested that fundamental hope discloses itself most tellingly when all of our specific "hopes" seem, for a time, to have collapsed. This hope, too, must of necessity be a gift of the Holy Spirit.

Robert Altman's film *Nashville* is a typical example of a story of the Lifegiver that nourishes our sense of fundamental hope. This brilliant contribution to our bicentennial celebration of independence makes our country music capital a metaphor for America, and America itself from its Puritan beginnings has been an image of the pilgrim people's progress toward the ideal of the kingdom. The Fourth of July is both our remembrance of colonial liberation and our renewal of hope as a nation. In the film, Nashville is celebrating the return from a sanatorium of one of its high-strung stars, just as an unseen presidential candidate prepares to inaugurate his Replacement Party campaign with a rally at the city's replica of the Parthenon. Even those who are put off by country-and-western music will revel in this masterful, but gentle satire of—and tribute to—America's perennial capacity for surviving its political and cultural insanity. After the film's climactic assassination attempt, a would-be country-and-western star calms the crowd at the rally with an improvised song. Its refrain is ironically emblematic of our national resilience in the face of catastrophe: "You may say that I ain't free, but it don't worry me." We are free, and if we make the right decisions under the direction of the Holy Spirit, there is no catastrophe great enough to keep us from our God-given goal.

On a surer note, because there is no satire in it at all, is the sense of hope we associate with David O. Selznick's masterpiece *Gone with the Wind*, the epic story of the South's rise from defeat. It is still unquestionably the American film that wins more superlatives than any other and for good reason—the most popular, the best-remembered, the most-widely seen (even though, in the age of inflated ticket costs, many have recently made more money) and, some still feel, Hollywood's greatest artistic achievement. Though it needs little introduction, a few observations may help to demonstrate its rightful place as a story of the Lifegiver. Scarlett O'Hara survives the Civil War, the burning of Atlanta, and two short marriages before she finally succumbs to the charms of Rhett Butler as part of her plan to survive Reconstruction. Scarlett and Rhett are the screen's most famous lovers; their on-again, off-again relationship (because of Scarlett's lingering infatuation for the husband of her cousin Melanie) is a poignant reminder of our unfinished human condition. Her instinct for survival amid adversity, rarely by ethical means, makes her a suitable reflector of the worldly steward of Jesus' parable, who is applauded by his master for acting cleverly in his own interest. As St. Luke explains, "the worldly are more astute than the other-worldly in dealing with their own kind" (Luke 16:8). Moreover, the film's narrative rhythm of reversal and renewal, of setback and survival, sustains our assumption that this American classic is the quintessential cinematic representation of fundamental hope. "After all," Scarlett reminds us, in the film's memorable last line, "tomorrow *is* another day."

There would seem to be no better way to end our treatment of stories of the Lifegiver than to recall the final image of Hopkins's poem "God's Grandeur," quoted in its entirety at the end of Part One. Although it seems primarily to be about creation, there is no doubt that it also suggests the new creation. The reason that "there lives the dearest freshness deep down things" and that "morning, at the brown brink eastward, springs," Hopkins firmly believes, is because the Holy Spirit embraces the world with his life-renewing powers: the warmth of his breast and the brightness of his wings. On one level, the poet celebrates the cycle of daily renewal, night to day. On another, he seems to suggest the end of history and the dawn of the new creation. It is not just the physical world that the Spirit renews; it is also the "bent" or sinful world that the Spirit, in the traditional image of a dove, nurtures back to wholeness. Once again, we attend to the freshness of the poet's own images:

> And though the last lights off the black West went
> Oh, morning, at the brown brink eastward, springs—
> Because the Holy Ghost over the bent
> World broods with warm breast and with ah! bright wings.

The superficial and the slipshod have ready answers, but those look-ing this complex life straight in the eye acquire a wealth of perception so composed of delicately balanced contradictions that they dread, or resent, the call to couch any part of it in a bland generalization. The vanity (if not outrage) of trying to cage this dance of atoms in a single definition may give the weariness of age with the cry of youth for answers the appearance of boredom.

—Peter De Vries, *The Blood of the Lamb*

Conclusion:
Tomorrow Comes

This attempt to demonstrate the manner in which fiction—both litera-ture and film—can nourish our faith began with an epigraph from Paul Tournier's *The Meaning of Persons*. A Christian psychiatrist's penetrating insights into personal wholeness, it is, I think, a classic of twentieth-century spirituality. The passage I quoted seemed especially appropriate to my purpose because it appeals to the manner in which God in three Persons enters into our history. It also rightly claims that it is "*above all* through the Bible . . . that God speaks" to us (my emphasis). To begin an ending, therefore, I want to affirm an assumption that this book, too, is built on, namely that the Bible is *the* principal book in our lives, but it is not and should not be the only one. There are many other texts available to us— short stories, novels, poems, plays, and films—that serve wonderfully to reflect the values, inspiration, and revelation of the Bible. As a variation on the earlier quotation from Peter De Vries, these other narratives, I like to think, become for us in our quest for mature belief the many, often complex reflections of our story of faith that enhance our appreciation of the "single definition" of the Apostles' Creed.

What should have emerged from our treatment of fiction in this book, I hope, is a way of approaching the continuing discernment of literature and film that supports the vision of the world that is central to Christian-ity. Ideally, the reader will go on to discover many other literary and cinematic analogies to the significance for our lives of the articles of the Apostles' Creed. I have, of course, by no means exhausted the possibilities of works that are capable of nourishing adult faith.

What is common to all of the stories that we have mentioned here is that they represent fictional worlds that convey a sense of hope. This does not mean that they all have happy endings—far from it in some cases. But it does imply that the writer or director imagines a world that is still open to possibilities, a world that is built on the belief that human beings are capable of change, even radical transformation, and thus a world that has a future. Now to a certain extent, as Harvard theologian Harvey Cox explains in his book *For Christ's Sake* (a title that seems to me regrettably trendy), hope is common to all varieties of religious expression:

> Our American religions are deeply infected with the moralistic and
> anti-festive qualities of industrial society. The truth is that in religion,
> dance precedes dogma; saturnalia comes before sermon. Man is *festive*.
> He thrives on parties, *fiestas*, holidays, breaks in his routine, times for
> toasting, singing the old songs, remembering and hoping. Also, man is a
> *fantasizer*. He keeps on dreaming of a world free of napalm and cancer
> and hunger, despite centuries of frustration. He won't stop hoping.

We celebrate, we imagine better worlds; in short, we hope. And, as Christians, our ultimate hope has a definite shape: the resurrection of the body
and life everlasting.

Insofar as drama developed in Greece out of religious celebrations—
in song and dance—it seems appropriate to turn to the stage for our last
story of hope. After decades of theatrical offerings that were at best minimal in inspiration, the world stage was in the late 1980s blest, in my opinion,
with the appearance of a show that in many ways sums up in its fictional
worldview the significance for our lives of the whole Apostles' Creed. I am
thinking, of course, of the Boublil-Schonberg production of *Les Miserables*.
Victor Hugo's 1862 novel that the musical is based on is a masterpiece of
world literature and deserves of course to be read for faith's nourishment
in its own right. There have, moreover, been at least five film adaptations,
the most accessible on tape being the 1978 made-for-TV version directed
by Glenn Jordan. The Broadway musical, however, charms the imagination and uplifts the spirit beyond comparison. I have chosen to conclude
this survey of fiction that nourishes faith with this production of *Les
Miserables* precisely because, as I have implied, it is a story of the Trinity:
Creator, Savior, and Lifegiver.

The hero of the story is Jean Valjean, whose history as a convict clearly
makes him a true Misfit, as Flannery O'Connor used the title in "A Good
Man Is Hard to Find." His punishments have never fit his crimes against
society, if his initial offense can be considered a crime in any sense at all—
only, it would seem, in the grossly unjust society that early
nineteenth-century France is presented as being. For stealing a loaf of bread
to feed his starving sister and her family, he is sentenced to five years in
prison! It is clearly a world in which the poor have little or no choice but
to take from those who have in abundance if they are to survive. Moral
theology would justify Valjean's act as a kind of occult compensation. The
musical drama begins when Valjean is paroled after serving nineteen years

on a chain gang, his term increased because of his attempts to escape from jail. In prison, Valjean proves himself to be a man of extraordinary physical strength, surely the play's metaphor for the spiritual strength that he comes to possess.

Valjean's conversion begins as the result of an act of forgiveness that is also a perfect image of God's compassionate mercy. Angered by his prison experience and unable to find lodging or food, he is befriended by the Bishop of Digne, whose kindness Valjean repays by stealing some silver. Apprehended by the police and returned with the stolen goods, Valjean is protected by the saintly cleric, who insists that the silver was a gift, adding two candlesticks for good measure. This experience of God's abundant mercy alters the course of Valjean's life, convincing him that the best way to repay the bishop is to follow his example. Although this scene, like so many in *Les Miserables*, conveys a sense of the whole creed's meaning for us—of life's benevolent purpose, of forgiveness and salvation, and of love's life-giving power—it primarily reflects our response to God as Creator inasmuch as it confirms our belief that God can and does draw good even from our mistakes.

Although the heart of the story has many melodramatic twists, the changed Valjean is such an endearing personality that all the elements fall into place and are, it seems to me, dramatically convincing and emotionally satisfying as well as faith-inspiring. Valjean's response to compassionate mercy is to become a defender of the poor in body and in spirit. To signal his new life, Valjean changes his name to Monsieur Madeleine and, before long, he reappears as the owner of a factory and the mayor of his town. In befriending a desperate and dying worker, Fantine, he promises to adopt her illegitimate child, Cosette. As the girl's adoptive father, Valjean repeatedly puts his life on the line; he is obviously her savior and a savior figure for the audience. His name change, however, had been a parole violation and, as a result, he is relentlessly pursued by Inspector Javert, whose obsessive devotion to blind justice becomes a dramatic focus for the musical's portrayal of society's evils. Valjean even saves Javert's life during the students' climactic, but futile revolt against injustice to the poor; the demonic Javert is finally unable to live with the memory of such a kindness.

In the last scene, love and forgiveness are presented as the ultimate gifts of the life-giving Spirit. As Jean Valjean lies dying with Cosette at his side, her mother, Fantine, appears to invite him to join those who have died in the course of the drama. The resplendent chorus of the "saints" moves slowly forward, from upstage center, to embrace Valjean. "Come with me," Fantine extends her hand, "Where chains will never bind you./ All your grief/ At last, as last, behind you./ Lord in Heaven,/ Look down on him in mercy." After Valjean's brief, final prayer for forgiveness, Eponine, who had given her life at the Paris barricades to save the life of a student she loved, separates herself from the approaching ranks of the dead, and joins Valjean and Fantine in the show's poignant climactic trio. Valjean offers his hand to Fantine and Eponine, to be led into salvation, as together they proclaim in unison the ennobling theme of the musical: "Take my love,/ For love is everlasting./ And remember/ The truth that once was spoken,/ To love another person/ Is to see the face of God." This is, of course, a variation on the lesson of the First Letter of John: "Though God has never been seen by any man, God himself dwells in us if we love one another" (1 John 4:12).

The lyrics of the final triumphant chorus of *Les Miserables* are surely some of the most moving ever heard on the contemporary stage; its rousing utopian images fuse the play's themes of love and compassion on earth, and freedom everlasting:

Do you hear the people sing
Lost in the valley of the night?
It is the music of a people
Who are climbing to the light.
For the wretched of the earth
There is a flame that never dies.
Even the darkest night will end
And the sun will rise.
They will live again in freedom
In the garden of the Lord.
They will walk behind the plough-share,
They will put away the sword.
The chain will be broken
And all men will have their reward. . . .
Will you join in our crusade?
Who will be strong and stand with me?
Somewhere beyond the barricade
Is there a world you long to see?
Do you hear the people sing
Say, do you hear the distant drums?
It is the future that they bring

When tomorrow comes . . .
Tomorrow comes!

The concluding words of the chorus—"Tomorrow comes!"—do more than suggest the faith implied in John's final exclamation in the Book of Revelation (22:20). They are fiction's perfect equivalent of the Bible's ultimate expression of hope:

"Come, Lord Jesus!"

Appendix

List of works treated and others recommended

(Note: Films are identified by the director's name, preceded by the abbreviation "Dir.," which is particularly helpful where literary works have been adapted for the screen without a change in name.)

Faith and Fiction: An Introduction

A Man for All Seasons (Robert Bolt)
A Man for All Seasons (Dir., Fred Zinnemann)

Part I: Stories of the Creator

God the Caring Father: Personal Sense of Belonging
"The River" (Flannery O'Connor)
The Member of the Wedding (Carson McCullers)
The Member of the Wedding (Dir., Fred Zinnemann)

Cosmic Sense of Belonging
Stagecoach (Dir., John Ford)
La Strada (Dir., Federico Fellini)
Grand Canyon (Dir., Lawrence Kasdan)

The Provident Creator: Shared Dominion under God
Genesis 1–2:14
"A Circle in the Fire" (Flannery O'Connor)
The Grapes of Wrath (John Steinbeck)
The Grapes of Wrath (Dir., John Ford)

Other Recommended Works
On the Waterfront (Dir., Elia Kazan)
Sounder (Dir., Martin Ritt)
Norma Rae (Dir., Martin Ritt)
Places in the Heart (Dir., Robert Benton)

Stewardship Limited by Mortality
Epic of Gilgamesh
Seize the Day (Saul Bellow)
"A Good Man Is Hard to find" (Flannery O'Connor)

Other Recommended Works
   As I Lay Dying (William Faulkner)
   The Violent Bear It Away (Flannery O'Connor)
   Steel Magnolias (Dir., Herbert Ross)
   Terms of Endearment (Dir., James Brooks)

Stewardship Hindered by Sin
Genesis 2:15–3
All About Eve (Dir., Joseph Mankiewicz)
All the King's Men (Robert Penn Warren)
All the King's Men (Dir., Robert Rossen)
East of Eden (John Steinbeck)
East of Eden (Dir., Elia Kazan)

Other Recommended Works
   The Catcher in the Rye (J. D. Salinger)
   A Separate Peace (John Knowles)
   Lord of the Flies (William Golding)
   Ordinary People (Judith Guest)
   Ordinary People (Dir., Robert Redford)

Structures of Sin: Depleting Natural and Human Resources
Saving Private Ryan (Dir., Steven Spielberg)
The Thin Red Line (Dir., Terrence Malick)
The Mission (Dir., Roland Joffe)
Slaughterhouse-Five (Dir., George Roy Hill)

Responses to the Goodness of Creation: Wonder and Gratitude
Close Encounters of the Third Kind (Dir., Steven Spielberg)
Empire of the Sun (Dir., Steven Spielberg)
The Right Stuff (Dir., Philip Kaufman)
"God's Grandeur" & "Pied Beauty" (Gerard Manley Hopkins)

Part II: Stories of the Savior

Representations of Jesus and Stories of the Savior
Jesus of Montreal (Dir., Denys Arcand)

Works Briefly Noted
   The King of Kings (Dir., Cecil B. DeMille)
   Jesus of Nazareth (Dir., Franco Zeffirelli)
   The Gospel According to Saint Matthew (Dir., Pier Paolo Pasolini)
   The Last Temptation of Christ (Dir., Martin Scorsese)
   Jesus Christ Superstar (Dir., Norman Jewison)
   Godspell (Dir., David Greene)

     Quo Vadis? (Dir., Mervyn LeRoy)
     The Robe (Dir., Henry Koster)
     Ben-Hur (Dir., William Wyler)

Passion: Redemptive Value of Unavoidable Suffering

     Cool Hand Luke (Dir., Stuart Rosenberg)
     The Outlaw Josey Wales (Dir., Clint Eastwood)
     The Last Picture Show (Dir., Peter Bogdanovich)

    Works Briefly Noted
      High Noon (Dir., Fred Zinnemann)
      Shane (Dir., George Stevens)
      Casablanca (Dir., Michael Curtiz)
      Serpico (Dir., Sidney Lumet)

Death: Self-Sacrifice in Remembrance of Him

     The Moviegoer (Walker Percy)
     Mass Appeal (Dir., Glenn Jordan)
     The Violent Bear It Away (Flannery O'Connor)
     Love in the Ruins (Walker Percy)
     The Thanatos Syndrome (Walker Percy)

Resurrection: Images of Liberation

     On the Waterfront (Dir., Elia Kazan)
     The Power and the Glory (Graham Greene)
     The Fugitive (Dir., John Ford)
     The Grapes of Wrath (Dir., John Ford)
     One Flew Over the Cuckoo's Nest (Ken Kesey)
     One Flew Over the Cuckoo's Nest (Dir., Milos Forman)
     Midnight Cowboy (Dir., John Schlesinger)
     E.T.: The Extraterrestrial (Dir., Steven Spielberg)

    Other Recommended Works
      Spartacus (Dir., Stanley Kubrick)
      Gandhi (Dir., Richard Attenborough)
      Beauty and the Beast (Dir., Gary Trousdale, Kirk Wise)

Life between Two Comings: Parables of Judgment

     Crimes and Misdemeanors (Dir., Woody Allen)
     To Kill a Mockingbird (Harper Lee)
     To Kill a Mockingbird (Dir., Robert Mulligan)
     La Dolce Vita (Dir., Federico Fellini)
     "A Good Man Is Hard to Find" (Flannery O'Connor)
     "Good Country People" (Flannery O'Connor)

"The Artificial Nigger" (Flannery O'Connor)
"Revelation" (Flannery O'Connor)

Part III: Stories of the Lifegiver

Gifts of the Spirit: Living with and through Others
"The Enduring Chill" (Flannery O'Connor)
It's a Wonderful Life (Dir., Frank Capra)
Leap of Faith (Dir., Richard Pearce)

Works Briefly Noted and Recommended
Mr. Deeds Goes to Town (Dir., Frank Capra)
You Can't Take It with You (Dir., Frank Capra)
Mr. Smith Goes to Washington (Dir., Frank Capra)
Auntie Mame (Dir., Morton DaCosta)
Star Wars (Dir., George Lucas)
Life Is Beautiful (Dir., Roberto Benigni)

Holy Catholic Church: Life-Giving Rituals
The Last Gentleman (Walker Percy)
"A Temple of the Holy Ghost" (Flannery O'Connor)
It Happened One Night (Dir., Frank Capra)
Bull Durham (Dir., Ron Shelton)
The Violent Bear It Away (Flannery O'Connor)
The Moviegoer (Walker Percy)

Other Recommended Works
The Wizard of Oz (Dir., Victor Fleming)
The Mission (Dir., Roland Joffe)
Mass Appeal (Dir., Glenn Jordan)
Keeping the Faith (Dir., Edward Norton)
Saving Grace (Dir., Robert M. Young)
When Harry Met Sally (Dir., Rob Reiner)
Tomorrow (Dir., Joseph Anthony)
As Good As It Gets (Dir., James Brooks)
The Lion King (Dir., Roger Allers, Rob Minkoff)

Communion of Saints: Here and Hereafter
The Grapes of Wrath (Dir., John Ford)
On the Waterfront (Dir., Elia Kazan)
Places in the Heart (Dir., Robert Benton)

Works Briefly Noted
Witness (Dir., Peter Weir)
Alice's Restaurant (Dir., Arthur Penn)

Forgiveness of Sins: Personal Transformation
    The Parable of the Prodigal Son (Luke 15:11–32)
    The Godfather: Part III (Dir., Francis Ford Coppola)
    Dead Man Walking (Dir., Tim Robbins)
    Grand Canyon (Dir., Lawrence Kasdan)
    The African Queen (Dir., John Huston)

    Works Briefly Noted and Recommended
        The Searchers (Dir., John Ford)
        Tender Mercies (Dir., Bruce Beresford)
        As Good As It Gets (Dir., James Brooks)

Resurrection of the Body: Hope Confirmed
    Resurrection (Dir., Daniel Petrie)
    "Pigeon Feathers" (John Updike)
    "Judgement Day" (Flannery O'Connor)

Life Everlasting: Reflections of Fundamental Hope
    Close Encounters of the Third Kind: The Special Edition (Dir., Steven
        Spielberg)
    Nashville (Dir., Robert Altman)
    Gone With the Wind (Dir., Victor Fleming)
    "God's Grandeur" (Gerard Manley Hopkins)

Conclusion: Tomorrow Comes

    Les Miserables (Alain Boublil & Claude-Michel Schonberg)

    Other Recommended Works
        Les Miserables (Victor Hugo)
        Les Miserables (Dir., Claude Chabrol)
        Les Miserables (Dir., Glenn Jordan)

Index